Ted Lewis

Novelist, Artist, Musician

Hard or Soft Boiled

Monty Martin

Dedicated to Dr John Ball
for his support of Ted Lewis

First edition published in 2015 by Barton Muse,

Second edition published in 2017 by Muse Publishing,
1 Soutergate, Barton upon Humber, North Lincolnshire DN18 5HG.

The cover photograph was taken from the flat roof of the former David Lee Photography studio on George Street prior to the adding of a second floor.

ISBN 13 9780993406010??

Designed by Reflex Graphic Design - 01225 832551

Printed and bound by Systematic Print Management Limited
T 01472 851091 www.systematicprint.com

Acknowledgments

Without inspiration and help this book would not have been possible. I am particularly grateful to the following:

Dr John Ball, Ted Lewis's caring friend and GP, who introduced me to Ted Lewis, for his interest, information and fellowship.

Dr John Dickinson, Ted's lifetime friend, and Mrs Nadine Dickinson, for spending time with me, providing invaluable information, sharing Ted's portrait of Nadine, reviewing my 2015 text and their lifetime concern for Ted.

Neil Ashley, Ted Lewis's friend, for his fellowship, provision of photographs and information.

Hon Toby Eady OBE, Ted's literary agent and sometime literary advisor to Ted Lewis's Estate.

Geoff Bryant, writer, lecturer and historian, who kindly read the 2015 manuscript and advised.

Jez Stewart, Curator (Animation) of the British Film Institute National Archive.

Vivian Halas of Halas and Batchelor.

Brian Greene for his initial interest in the life of Ted Lewis, his research and writings.

Nick Cole of the *Scunthorpe Telegraph* for his continued interest and press features.

Zilla Gilfoy, who has always been an inspiration and on hand to provide information and photographs. She also kindly read through my 2015 the text.

Joan Barton, who helped with early research and encouraged me to form the Ted Lewis Group.

Nick Triplow, journalist and biographer of Ted Lewis, especially for his radio contributions, video screenplay and writings.

Sean O'Brien, for his understanding of Ted Lewis and his contributions to a radio documentary.

Moira Trafford, who has spent many hours patiently undertaking much proofreading and discussing the text.

Nick Turner, one of Ted's boyhood friends, for his time and fellowship, information, support and invaluable text reviews.

Jill Turner, Nick's wife, for introducing me to her husband many years ago and for her support.

James Usher for his enthusiasm, manuscript reading, work with the Ted Lewis Group and generously painting a truly inspired posthumous portrait of Ted Lewis, which was the cover for the 2015 edition.

Jackie Usher, for research, proofreading, work with the Ted Lewis Group and encouragement.

Kathy Hill and Danielle Smith of MD Signs in Barton upon Humber, for their creative committed work on graphics.

Richard Ireland, for his creative and helpful design.

Ron Burnett, former trombonist with Unity Jazz Band, a friend of Ted Lewis who kindly helped me with much Unity Jazz Band and other history, providing photographs, literature and artefacts.

Judy Burnett, Ron's wife and former student at Hull College of Art and Design.

Lance Waddell, who introduced me to others that remember Ted in his Hull student days.

Jane Marlin, for the use of Lewis's painting of Unity Jazz Band.

Phil Corby, who introduced me to Lance Waddell, for his enthusiasm after being involved in readings from Ted's novels.

June and Ian Barnett, who hosted my initial readings of *The Rabbit* and *Jack's Return Home* at The Old Mill during Barton Arts Festivals.

Ted Lewis Group members not mentioned elsewhere, especially Rose Lennon and Carol Thornton.

Barton Civic Society for its contributions and custodianship of Ted Lewis's sketches.

Ian Wolseley and Wilderspin National School for their unfailing support.

The Queen Street School Preservation Trust, particularly for the enthusiasm and work of Paul Thornton, which has offered to accommodate a permanent Ted Lewis Memorial and Study Centre.

Jim and Sarah Woodhouse of The George Inn, formerly The George Hotel, one of Ted Lewis's watering holes.

Lila Harrison, now sadly passed away, thirty-five years in charge of Lila's Bar at The George Hotel, Barton upon Humber, a friend of Ted Lewis, and who provided me with much background and encouragement.

Maggie Robinson, Neil Storey, Nancy Hornsby, Hella Johnson, Mally Speck, Betty Griffiths, Russ Harrison, Barbara Hewson, Pauline Such, David Tidswell, Eric Babington, Heather Brown, Ida Lee, Barry Atkinson, Dave Mouncey, Roger Sharpless, Jonah Lacey-Hatton, Sue Lacey-Hatton, Richard Scott OBE, Keri-Louise Lusby, Diane Cardee and countless other people who provided anecdotes, information, corrections or encouragement, and others whose names I may have inadvertently omitted.

David Lee and Brian Peeps, for help with archive photographs.

Hull History Centre.

John and June Fletcher.

Mark Verna in the USA, who has contributed magazine articles.

Alain Clément in France, who provided details of overseas translated publications.

Chris Ellis, owner of *Barton upon Humber and Surrounding Villages Memories* Facebook page, and many enthusiastic contributors to that page whose names are numerous, and are recorded there with comments and photographs.

Contributors to the *Ted (Get Carter) Lewis* Facebook page.

Anne Henderson, daughter of bandleader Harold Johnson, for information and for her contribution to 'the testosterone theory'.

The writings of Ted Lewis, now represented by his estate, in respect of extracts from the relevant novels, which have contributed to a better understanding of the author in this study.

Photographs

I acknowledge, to the best of my information and belief, the contribution of or permission to publish selected photographs and graphics, the sources of which are known, in the following illustration pages:

Page 43 Nick Turner and Neil Ashley

Page 44 Brian Peeps and Neil Turner

Page 45 Brian Peeps and Nancy Hornsby

Page 46 Neil Ashley

Page 47 Neil Ashley and Zilla Gilfoy

Page 48 Neil Ashley and Jane Marlin

Page 49 Neil Ashley, Ron Burnett and Hull City Council

Page 90 Jonah Lacy-Hatton and Ron Burnett

Page 92 Nancy Hornsby and Stephen J Parkes

Page 93 John Harrison and Nadine Dickinson

Page 94 Barton Civic Society

Page 95 Barton Civic Society

Page 96 Nancy Hornsby

I also acknowledge the originators of artwork whose identity has not been traced or inadvertently omitted despite diligent enquiry.

Foreword

My interest in Ted Lewis followed a brief fellowship visit to that author as he lay, very ill, in Scunthorpe General Hospital. Introduced by his GP, until then I had never heard of Ted Lewis nor seen the film *Get Carter.* I have no enthusiasm for crime, noir, gangster, or violent books or movies, but later read *The Rabbit*, a first edition of the largely autobiographical novel that Ted handed to me that day.

I lived then, as I do now, in Barton upon Humber, which was to all intents and purposes Ted Lewis's home town. In his novel, *The Rabbit*, Ted Lewis described life in that town and in Hull, when youth was finding itself during the 1950s. The novel is a compelling account of a student artist emerging from an artisan background, including a frank account of his exuberant teenage 1950s life; struggling, gauche loves; and escapades.

Reading more of Ted's work following his premature death at the age of forty-two, I became increasingly absorbed. I then purchased *Carter* from a second-hand book shop, which was the first paperback version of Lewis's novel, *Jack's Return Home*, published by Pan on the back of the film *Get Carter's* popular success. Later editions called the novel *Get Carter*. I was later privileged to read the full text of both this book and that of *The Rabbit* to audiences at Barton's Old Mill as part of the Barton Arts Festivals. At these events, others expressed an interest and volunteered fascinating cameos of the novelist. In this way, the Ted Lewis Group was born. Full of enthusiasm, I wrote a first edition of this book, which was at once raw and instinctive, containing hesitating sketches of a man who was himself a master of caricature and whom I knew incompletely. That first edition has sold out to buyers locally, nationally and internationally, prompting further insights from many sources, including information derived from exhibitions and social media. Much later, I was told that one Christmas, Ted had dined in our small restaurant in Barton, but sadly I did not see him there.

I continue to be grateful to so many of Ted's friends and acquaintances, as well as members of the Ted Lewis Group, who have provided personal information and encouragement without which this edition would not have been possible. I hope you will enjoy it, and feel free to provide any other information you feel could be useful to establish an accurate picture of the remarkable Ted Lewis, author, artist and musician, whose life was all too short.

Monty Martin

No Return for Ted Lewis

I was watching out of the windscreen, perched uncertainly on the edge of a well-worn, plush, cream-leather passenger seat in John's special equipment, gold-metallic-painted luxury saloon of a certain yet treasured age.

Our destination was Scunthorpe; in 1982, its future uncertain, as it was no longer the dominant Lincolnshire steel town it had been. Just six years earlier, British Steel Corporation had demolished the smoking, seemingly haphazard smelters, furnaces, hoppers, 'Crazy Legs' cranes, trucks, notices, prohibited areas and all other detritus of the once proud Peter Lysaght's mile-long Normanby Park steelworks. In its place was a community project of land reclamation, complete with a site for travellers who then proceeded to wreck that as well. Steel production was confined just to the Appleby-Frodingham Anchor Plant, which dominated the eastern entry to the town, a construction that had been scarred by engineering, not of industrial plant, but by fictitious payments to a significant number of corrupt civil engineers and their acolytes.

Our route took us past Scunthorpe railway station with its entrance, unsurprisingly, in eponymous Station Road. Facing us at the traffic lights was a brick, Art Deco, clean-lined Post Office headquarters, which, on being built, had taken one look at the rest of the town and realised that elegance did not suit the area. Artistic and distinctive building style, or indeed any style at all, was therefore still-born in the town.

Running between that once-interesting building and the ancient St Lawrence Parish Church was Church Lane, one of the few leafy, respectable, middle-class areas to grace the town. We cruised slowly along, alert for a gap in a tightly parked procession of kerbside saloons, vans and occasional battered vans, some of which had squeezed onto grass verges in their eagerness to park, leaving ugly, brown ruts on grass verges: the bane of the neat front-garden-tending brigade.

"There's one, John."

We nearly passed an unexpected gap, which suddenly appeared in this determined nose-to-tail line of vehicles. The Jag pulled to a nonchalant halt.

"Sorry, I think it may be too small."

No reply.

Unhurriedly, the driver executed a perfectly judged reverse park. The driver's door opened with leisure, the driver carefully checking the vehicle's position. A seven-series BMW was immediately in front of it, an obviously treasured Triumph Stag behind. If 'Q' and his gadgets had been present we could have been part of a James Bond movie. I mused, full of film-fantasy ideas.

"I'm surprised some jobsworth's yellow lines haven't reached here," I exclaimed, but no one likes a smart-arse remark and there was no reply again. Come on, I'd only been making conversation.

We marched off purposefully past more and more lines of clogging vehicles, a sudden splash of blues and twos adding illumination to the emerging A & E sign, its reception now emerging from the gloom. To my surprise, having entered through wide, glass automatic doors, we could walk unchallenged down a corridor past reception. John was a GP, though, clearly an advantage as we strode along Scunthorpe General's blue-grey, unfriendly, seemingly endless yards of cold corridor.

It was visiting time. Up small narrow stairs, turning left and right, we encountered the occasional pre-occupied healthcare professional, once recognisably called doctors and nurses in less pretentious days. We steered round singles, couples and small groups with one thing in common – a hesitating search for specific wards or destinations, or even a way out, with their easy route disguised by oddly elusive signage and no prescient hope of help.

The patient was pale, overweight and listless in bed with an unspoken debilitating condition requiring a drip. John greeted him as 'Ted', the man I had been invited to see; told he was a writer with problems – could I help to lift the low mood that was leaking self-worth and delaying a much-needed recovery? It had been unspoken between John and me that there were areas of my life somewhat in common with Ted – taking a nonchalant view of life with happy boozing, regretting past unsuccessful marriages, happily avoiding others and an eclectic interest in jazz. John had also told me that Ted had an easy facility to rub shoulders with petty crooks, gangsters, women on the make and ne'er-do-wells. So did I but rarely read the kind of crime novels like *Jack's Return Home* John told me the patient wrote.

From the bed, slightly watery eyes were seeking something far into the distance; an instant sign that our palliative objective would be no easy task as Ted seemed intuitively to recognise my self-doubt. John and I both attended Trinity Methodist Church in our town of Barton upon Humber:

the North Lincolnshire market town that had carelessly lost its market. However, any faith we still clung on to did not appear to be a useful tool for this visit. The knowing, blue eyes of Ted Lewis, novelist, jazz musician and graphic artist, continued to hold mine, scrutinising without expression on his face. As his cousin, Alf Lewis, once observed, *"He looked at me as an inconvenience."*

After a stilted introduction and some initial pleasantries, we mutually recognised that 'you can't kid the kidder', so the depth of our pleasantries was circumscribed much as a bar-room chat between strangers is until booze loosens self-consciousness. Intrusive rasping coughs came from a hidden, huddled form in a bed opposite. In between his own bouts of breathlessness, Ted hinted briefly at despair, but later we went on to less poignant topics – our mutual town, the weather, Scunthorpe United and the National Health Service.

After some time, when the visit was in danger of becoming something of a charade, I was pleased to hear John caution that his patient was tiring. We rose to say our goodbyes; our real objective hardly touched upon. Much later, reading Ted's first, 1965, novel, the following words had particular resonance: *"I was glad when it was time to go. Not because of the banal conversation, because I find I'm very good at it and quite enjoy it, but because I was glad to be getting away from being scrutinised, whatever the verdict."*

I was destined never to see Ted Lewis alive again. Before we left, he pressed into my hands a copy of *The Rabbit*, a kind gift and his familiar one for acquaintances. I was then no avid reader of fiction for law books took a toll of my limited concentration on the written word, being tools of my professional survival and income. I turned the book over in my hands and gave him short but polite thanks, little realising that it was a first edition or that it would become a trigger to fire me into a search for the real art, life and times of Ted Lewis.

I failed in the one vital objective of our visit, which was to bring comfort and hope to that needful, depressed, multi-talented artist who was feeling a failure. Later, his debilitating health did not allow him the strength to reach The Wheatsheaf, or keep up with the rounds and stories of its regulars. Maybe my later efforts to keep his art alive is a belated apology.

Chapter 1

The Importance of Being Ted Lewis

Had there been no ready purchaser for the film rights to Lewis's novel *Jack's Return Home*, as a basis for the seminal 1971 film Get Carter, there might have been no studies of his life's work. However, that innovative novel, which has been feted as one of the best British, hard-boiled, criminal thrillers ever written, is a secure peg on which to hang the story of Ted Lewis's life, work and times, which more recently would have conferred celebrity status upon him. Initially released to critics' lukewarm responses, *Get Carter* properly grew in mass-audience appreciation, achieving iconic recognition. Even now it still sells as a DVD, and the programmed repeats on terrestrial TV have the regularity of Jack Carter's casual female conquests.

Jack's Return Home was the second of Lewis's nine novels, seven of which demonstrate the author's acute understanding of the criminal underworld. Their stories roll along as surely as the reels of the feature films that Lewis avidly watched and that often provided him with inspiration. Whilst two of those novels were semi-autobiographical, *Jack's Return Home* was a foundation, inspiration and source of a new British 'noir' writing style, which represents Lewis's importance going forward.

'Noir' writing characteristically features an amoral main character who muscles his or her way through a usually seedy, violent series of events, often involving sexual promiscuity or abuse. These characteristics are quite different from the earlier eyebrow-lifting humour in Leslie Charteris's *Saint* novels; the crusading, nationalist zeal of Ian Fleming's *James Bond*, with his schoolboy-mind gadgets; or the faux tough-guy romance of spaghetti westerns. Until Ted Lewis, 1960s aficionados of the hard-boiled crime novel could find it mainly from American toughies, such as Raymond Chandler and Micky Spillane.

Whilst there had been a UK noir tradition in the 1930/40s from writers such as Eric Ambler and Graham Greene, there was then a hiatus in such writing until 1970. Whether this was good, bad or indifferent depends on the reader's taste in crime or action fiction. However, no matter the style or subject, it is his recognisable, distinct, compelling prose that singles out Ted Lewis as not only a revivalist and entertaining writer but a novelist of singular importance and distinction.

Yet writing was not Ted Lewis's only talent or even the first to emerge. From an early age, he showed a prodigious flair for drawing; his expertise at sixteen being of a sufficient standard to enable him to gain admission to a diploma course in graphic art at Hull College of Arts and Crafts. Accordingly, Lewis's initial career path began in commercial art. Lewis was also a pianist who soon developed a syncopated style that led, not only to a passion for mainly modern or mainstream jazz but also included an ability to play 'trad' or New Orleans jazz in the rhythm section of Hull's Unity Jazz Band. Later in life, he entertained others informally, but only when the mood took him.

There were four main influences in Lewis's writings: Barton upon Humber (Barton), its topography and people; the writer, poet and teacher, Henry Treece; a love and understanding of action films, particularly the noir genre; and, finally, his time amongst the 'fleshpots' of Soho. All these melded together to yield novels that grip, entertain and stand the test of time,

Although we know the novelist best as Ted Lewis, he was called Edward, Ed, Eddie, Lew, Lewis or Ted depending on the time of his life and the people who chose to use these appellations, and therefore he is referred to by those different names depending on the time of his life or the people he was in contact with. It is from his two semi-autobiographical novels, *All the Way Home and All the Night Through*h and *The Rabbit*, that we can see, through his eyes and words, how these early progressions in life made the man and it is from the novelist's own words that we can achieve most insight into what truly mattered to him.

Chapter 2

All Through the Early Days

1940 to 1952

Edward Alfred 'Ted' Lewis, a World War II child, was born on 15th January 1940 at home, 5 Barkway Road in the Manchester conurbation of Stretford. He was registered with the name of Alfred Edward Lewis in the Stretford Registration Sub-district of Barton, somewhat ironically, given the name of the town, Barton upon Humber, where he eventually settled.

Throughout life, Ted Lewis used his registered forenames in reverse order. His father was Henry Lewis (always known as Harry), who was a ships' brokers clerk, and his mother was Bertha (formerly Bertha Shaw). They married at St Peter's Church in Stretford in 1935, fairly late in life when both were aged twenty-six, and before World War II changed lives and the world forever.

When Harry was called up to serve in the Royal Air Force, initially as an Aircraftsman 2, Bertha (then aged thirty-one) was left on her own to bring up their child. When Harry was demobbed they were both thirty-six, and had no further children. There is no doubt that Bertha was a loving mother, so their child was central to both her and, later, Harry's affections. The first family home was at 5 Barkway Road, Stretford; a respectable, 1920s, semi-detached, Lancashire house in a large area of indistinguishable suburban-style houses. Their son was not strong, having contracted rheumatic fever, a condition which deeply concerned the parents and affected the boy's early life.

After being demobbed, Harry was part of a bewildered workforce, many disabled physically and mentally, facing a labour market that had been taken over by women, and men of advancing years. Fortunately, Harry secured work, reputedly through a contact in the Manchester Ship Canal Company, as a quarry manager for the mining company, Singleton Birch in Melton Ross, but this entailed the family moving across the country to Lincolnshire. Harry's pre-war job was not, however, in the same area of expertise as his pre-war or service occupations.

Melton Ross is 14 miles east of the then mainly fishing port of Grimsby and west of the predominantly agricultural market town of Brigg, all three of which are linked by the A18 trunk road running east to west parallel to but some 15 miles south of the Humber Estuary. There was only one road crossing to the East Yorkshire bank of the Humber, which was via the Boothferry swing bridge near Goole, some 54 miles distant from Melton Ross. The other method of travel to East Yorkshire was the Humber Ferry, which was to feature significantly in two of Ted Lewis's books.

Harry's first workplace was not only at Singleton Birch's vast Melton Bottom chalk pit but also at the quarry, called a lime pit, cut into the Wolds just outside the small village of Elsham, which itself was about 8 miles distant from the Melton Ross. That estate village is situated on the edge of the Lincolnshire Wolds, halfway between Brigg on the A18 and Barton upon Humber, which is a town to the north of Brigg, situated at the end of the Lincolnshire Wolds as they descend into the Humber Estuary. Elsham grew up around its seventeenth-century hall, which, in 1946, became the residence of the Elwes family. For the convenience of that hall, the Victorians built a railway station, now unused, but which became essential to transport chalk and stones from the quarry. There is now only a level crossing and signal box where the station once served the area; the gates often closed to the thunder of dark, interminable goods or clattering passenger trains because this line remains the busy and important line between Grimsby and Doncaster. Atop the Wolds, above the village, was a World War II airfield, which would have been of interest to Harry in view of his war service in the RAF, although it later became a disused and ultimately dreary hulk. By contrast, Capt. Elwes, who had undertaken considerable improvements to Elsham Hall, opened the grounds to visitors in 1970, but, by that time, Harry had died and his successful son was living in Suffolk.

In 1946, the Lewis family needed to find a convenient place to live in a strange area. Brigg and Barton upon Humber boasted thriving markets at the time, but Barton, as it is called locally, had more industry and, as now, cheaper and more available housing. It also had a history of quarrying for chalk and clay, raw materials that were manufactured into bricks, tiles and cement. Adjacent to the Humber Estuary, via train, and the Humber Ferry, Barton had access to Hull on the north bank of that estuary. It was in Barton that Harry looked for and found a suitable home for his family.

In the mid-1930s, Barton developer, Horace Foster, had built an estate of some thirty-two semi-detached homes in a cul-de-sac, some half a mile from the town centre, at the west end of West Acridge, a road leading from that centre into wide, open farmland. At the entrance to the estate were two more imposing detached residences, marking the area a cut above others nearer the town. Foster built these houses sturdily of traditional, local brick and tile, with modern transom windows, creating a varied, pleasing street scene. Open aspect front doors completed a sense of homeliness and community. Ted Lewis described the overall area in his first novel: *"There is a Westfield Road, an Eastfield Road, a West Acridge and an East Acridge. Old names abound; Castledyke, Fleetgate and Holydyke."* When Barton was predominantly rural, West Acridge was the pre-enclosure field area cultivated or grazed by residents in parcels or strips for their own sustenance, often in return for rent or services. A corresponding field, East Acridge, was at the other side of town.

Harry purchased the 1938, semi-detached, three-bedroomed house at 118 West Acridge, Barton upon Humber on 5th September 1946 from a first-time buyer, Mr H Bacon, so it was already decorated and had a lived-in feel. The deal was financed with the aid of a mortgage from the Co-operative Permanent Building Society. In those days, the husband traditionally owned the family home so Bertha, a wife for eleven years, did not have her name on the legal title. Interestingly, houses on the West End Estate were of a similar design to 5 Barkway Road, so the family would have felt comfortable with it. There the similarity with Stretford ended. Lancastrian Manchester consisted of large areas where buildings dominated, along with smoke, smell and crowds. Lincolnshire was mainly rural with some focussed areas of residence and discrete industry. Stretford boasted Manchester United's football club ground, Old Trafford, and Harry was a lifelong supporter: *"Manchester United ... the finest football club in the world."*. The Stretford area also included the Trafford Industrial Estate where some seventy-five thousand Lancastrians were employed. Barkway Road was in the density of a built-up area; West End Estate was essentially the rural extremity of a town, and many of its houses had originally been farms. However, 1950s Barton did have some industry, and was part of an essentially self-supporting and proud community as Ted Lewis later recorded, *"Hardly anyone ever leaves the place."* The sense of peace and belonging soon became part of the youngster's life in an environment he found fulfilling, which influenced his later writing, shaped his outlook and was the area to which he returned at the end of his days.

Moving house, especially to a different environment, is an upheaval at the best of times. Happily, the Lewises, Harry, Bertha and Edward, found Bartonians welcoming, and former neighbours speak of the family as friendly and contented. Number 118, in common with all West End Estate houses, had a small front garden planted with traditional ornamental flowers. Boundaries were marked with neat, new walls, some with regulation embryo privet hedges (before the greenery had time to decline through neglect and indifferent pruning into twiggy disreputability). Since cars were a rarity at the time, there was no space provided for garages on West End Estate, but each house included a modest back garden to enable the family to plant fruit and vegetables as a supplement to family meals. To the rear of 118 and its neighbouring houses was an unmade, rough lane, which later led to Foster's store and yard that was even later reborn as a small factory. The Lewises' house, therefore, had an uninterrupted view over a mile of open land to the dark, faintly forbidding, tidal Humber Estuary with another land, East Yorkshire, on the other side. Barges flooded the estuary, as well as military craft after the war, according to Richard Scott who lived at 159 West Acridge.

Young Ted Lewis, known then in the family as Edward or Eddie, slept in a small bedroom at the rear of number 118. From there, his young eyes could stare across farmlands, wide-open spaces, to the north and west, enjoying views of Greenwoods' and Simpsons' cultivated agricultural land with pasture for grazing cows and horses; rotated crops; the Liberal Club Football Club; the remnants of brick or tile manufacturers; and disused quarries. From six years of age, Ted had the benefit of a secure cul-de-sac environment with youngsters of his age to pal up with and, at the same time, a rural adventure playground; the track at the back of his house leading into farmland, where now there is a large estate of modern housing. Those few brick-and-tile pits that remained have largely now been taken over by the Lincolnshire Wildlife Trust; peaceful waters that are an ideal habitat for indigenous birds, as well as for migrants flying in from the Arctic and North European countries. All this became part of the boy's life in a short time.

The family soon discovered that Barton had been the centre of that tile- and brick-making industry because of its readily available alluvial clay. Before the Lewises' time, that Humber-bank industry had been vibrant when Barton was also a port and boats came into The Haven, a Waterside Area creek flowing into the town, affording walks down to the boatyard, a remnant of earlier, seafaring days. Nearer home, young Edward's extensive playground included Mr Pond's three-acre orchard to the south-east of the estate, providing a fertile scrumping ground for mischievous youngsters. Mr Pond was a redoubtable figure who rode his tricycle zig zag into any headwind, dressed distinctively in a bottle-green coat and knickerbockers. The orchard was ultimately purchased in the 1960s by the West End Estate developer, Foster, so he could supply fashionable, and now scarce, bungalows to eager buyers. Denys Field was then Horace Foster's apprentice, but eventually became a well-respected Barton builder. There is a legend that when he had become a renowned novelist Edward, then writing as Ted Lewis, invited Denys to a party given by fashionable writer and journalist, Jilly Cooper, introducing him as one of the north's gangsters. It has not been possible to secure a second source for this, but it is too good a linking story to ignore.

As the boys grew older they could be trusted to roam further abroad, and the fields and Humber Bank became magnets. Boyhood friend Nick Turner recalls that *"This pathway at the rear of the houses leading to Horace Foster's yard was our route to freedom. It took us out to the fields and quarries we loved to range over and play in without feeling restricted in way."* A sense of space and freedom, which was the area's most precious gift, stayed with Ted Lewis all his life, and enabled him to see the town he so loved in relation to the surrounding countryside and river setting. *"Small hills, caused by the downward, riverward sweep of the Wolds ... hedge trees and fields, skylines and horizons are just right in relationship to each other."* Edward's bedroom vistas were a godsend for him; a solace and companion as his rheumatic fever was still a problem and, in consequence, he spent many days, weeks and months there, acquiring an acute future artist's eye. Light glistened on Humber mud banks, which emerged, seal like, from the shallow channels of the estuary when the tide was out. Occasional pleasure yachts added to estuary traffic, giving movement when the waters were still, bleak and reflective. The bank of the estuary, green in spring and summer, was nevertheless dismal, with deep abandoned pits that pockmarked the lengthy shoreline, which no longer bustled with businesses that quarried for chalk or dug for clay.

Young Edward, soon palled up with other young boys on the estate, Martin and Nick Turner at number 134, John Dickinson across the road at 141 and Richard (Dick) Scott at the far end of the estate. The boys played in the street, often opposite number 118, as well has having effective free rein to rove over the open spaces as parents were less risk averse and abduction was unheard of. One danger was unspent ammunition or mines that had been left on exercises by American soldiers during the war, and Dick Scott remembers parents cautioning youngsters to be careful, whereas today they would probably have prohibited their children from going into the area.

Edward, known as Ed or Eddie to his friends, first attended Barton County Primary School, which had been built in 1914 on Castledyke, the road at the end of West Acridge, by the then Lindsey County Council and named Castle Dykes School. It is now much expanded, still educating young pupils and has embraced the name Castledyke School. Whilst there was almost certainly a castle in Barton in the twelfth century, built where the Old Mill Pub now stands (there is a Castledyke South and Holydyke in Barton as well), no remains of either castle or dyke remain. Ed and his pals took the ten-minute half-a-mile walk to school past the fields and wide estuary vista towards Barton town centre. Instead of carrying on to the High Street and the busy Fleetgate, which took you to the Waterside area of the town, Ed and his school friends would turn sharp left finding the school 100 yards further on, a safe and convenient walk from home.

There were no roads to cross for Ed and his friends on the walk to school. Despite a steady increase in motorised transport, children would encounter only a limited number of vehicles on the way to school, whereas Castledyke School is now on a busy one-way system, which, twice a day in term time, becomes congested with the additional vehicles of the parents collecting or delivering their children, despite road markings that prohibit parking.

Chapter 3

Barton upon Humber

'A town remembered in perpetual Kodachrome'

Ted Lewis's familiarity with and love for the new, free, rural area with its town facilities and social life grew and matured through early teenage years to adulthood. He achieved a depth of understanding of the environment and its characters through observation and involvement, effortlessly transmitting this in later writings.

In the 1950s, before, while and after the Lewis family moved to Barton, Britain was reeling from and wrestling with pre-war social attitudes and the heritage of economic restrictions, whereas today there is relative prosperity. Barton's centre still retains its essential layout of centuries past, its 'Mom and Pop' owned shops with fronts bolted onto former farms, as well as town houses from its Georgian or Victorian past, both grand and modest. However, the population since Ted Lewis's young days has doubled to twelve thousand, dominated by commuters earning their money elsewhere and spending it there too; an entirely changed demography though perching on the past. The most obvious general historical developments, to which Barton was no stranger, are the advent of the motor car, the rise of supermarkets, out of town shopping, prosperity, the decline in manufacturing, an increase in services, the Internet and increased expectations.

A picture of 1950s Barton upon Humber and surrounding areas helps to understand the local aspect of Ted Lewis's literature, remembering that, cheekily, Lewis changed names and descriptions on a whim, but not consistently. He was in good literary company. Charles Dickens, when he described personal moments, poignantly uses shame and filial loyalty in the delivery of food to his father in Marshalsea Debtors' Prison to flesh out the story of *Little Dorrit*. Dickens also had first-hand experience with the Chancery Division as a model for the Circumlocution Office, so tellingly recounted in *Bleak House*. Henry Miller's plays, including *Death of a Salesman*, are based on Miller's experiences as the son of a Jewish immigrant to America, recounting success transformed into later poverty during the Depression. 'Write what you know about' is a truthful literary cliché. Lewis, following the tried and tested advice, did so without banality or self-indulgence.

Lewis's descriptions compare quite directly with Alan Bennett's style when telling of his own home town: *"I do, on the other hand, notice the city. For all so much of Leeds is soot coloured and black there is an astonishing range of colour and texture in its brick and stone. The setts which pave so many of the streets (and, underneath the asphalt, still do) are for the most time greasy and black, but after a storm glow with the assorted colours of the stone, and even the acres of red brick and slate roof take on a richness and shine."*. By comparison, this is Ted Lewis's lyrical description of the town he loved is arguably of the same standard as Bennet's *"The town where my home is lies on the banks of a wide river. It's a small town, about six thousand souls all told. It slopes up from the flat marshland next to the river to the top of the healthy Wolds. The plan of the town hasn't changed much since feudal times."*

Author Ted Lewis, as we have seen, also described a town that was self-contained and provided employment for its residents. However, in reality, manufacturing in Barton had started to decline in the 1950s, but was still something of a force to be reckoned with. Hall's Barton Ropery's quarter-of-a-mile brick and pantile factory still employed many, and made ropes for shipping and other purposes. Associate Chemical Company (ACC), works thrived east of the Waterside area of Barton near the Humber bank. Earlier, the Farmer's Company, Albright and Wilson, and then, finally, as Britag (ICI) all contributed gross pollution in the area approached by Chemical Lane. Nevertheless, former acquaintance, David Tidswell remembers scavenging that area with his pal Ed to collect barley to feed their families' domestic chickens. Hopper's Cycle Works still employed up to four hundred workers in its Marsh Lane factory, and much of the population adjusted its activities to the twin hooters of Hoppers and Halls, both morning and afternoon. Barton had, and still has, some splendid Georgian houses and fine, imposing, Victorian public buildings consisting of a Primitive Methodist Chapel, Queen Street School (now Wilderspin National Museum School, which houses Ted Lewis's sketches of historic Barton), the Oddfellows' Hall, the police station, the magistrates' court and the Assembly Rooms (built as Barton's Temperance Hall).

For recreation, films were screened in two cinemas, and dances were held at the Drill Hall, now demolished, and the Assembly Rooms;

"two hours dancing and two hours fighting". The Harold Johnson Band was a popular early 1950s dance-hall entertainment, one line-up including Ted's friend Alan Dickinson as its trombonist. The best dance floor in the area, however, was on the first floor of Oddfellows' Hall; the ground floor of which prospered as a Friendly Society office, standing proudly on the High Street, whereas today it blinks through smashed windows. The Conservative Club (now the Corn Exchange Club) in the Market Place was where Barton's worthies gathered to play cards, snooker, put the world to rights and make deals. Pubs such as the Steam Packet (named after Barton's more glorious seagoing history), Coach and Horses, Red Lion, White Lion, George Hotel, Wheatsheaf, Volunteer Arms and Blue Bell all had their place in Bartonians' recreation, and often later in Ted Lewis's novels.

The closely-knit town's population felt secure *"Everybody has their problems, people there worry as much as anywhere else but the surface effect is one of easiness."* From a young age, Edward was aware of enlarged opportunities for Bartonians in East Yorkshire's 'City and County' of Kingston upon Hull, only a train/ferry journey away across the Humber. Indeed, those who lived in Barton's Waterside area, alongside The Haven, often found it preferable to travel by train and ferry to Hull. There they found better shopping and other entertainment perceived to be more exciting than in the centre of Barton. Ted Lewis, writing before the construction of the Humber Bridge recorded *"Some get office jobs with firms in the nearby cities and study accountancy in the evenings, travelling to work on the train or on the ferry ... only a few stay on at school in the sixth form and then go on to University or Training College. Some sail the barges up and down the river. Others go to sea."* In his 1971 novel, Plender, one of the principal characters had to drive round the end of the Humber Estuary to reach a hiding place in the Barton area in the absence of a suitable ferry.

Barton had a railway station at the end of the line, which was also important to Edward, his family and many others, but it was rather more imposing then than it is today; it was more commodious with traditional railway-style passenger buildings, properly staffed, with its perimeter marked by iron railings. There was a tradition that if you were looking for work or to hire casual labour, leaning on those railings was often a sign of availability, although a locomotive famously crashed the points and irreparably damaged them, much to the despair of that cameo labour market. In Ted Lewis's semi-autobiographical novel, *The Rabbit*, Victor Graves' father habitually picked up workers from the station and took them to work at the quarry he managed. The area is now called The Terminus, but the station's stylish buildings were removed in 1973 during Operation Eyesore (sic). Only a reduced length of the railings and a bare platform remain, and, in consequence, the once vibrant area has now lost its magic. Happily, The White Swan, which once boasted horses in adjacent stables, still dominates the area as it always has, and once briefly dominated the adult Lewis's romantic life in later times when it was the White Swan's landlady who became a more interesting, although illicit, attraction for Ted than its ale.

For Edward and others to reach Hull it was necessary catch a train on the then Barton Line. Rather than continuing to the seaside town of Cleethorpes on the northeast coast of Lincolnshire, he would alight at New Holland from where the ferry sailed. However, uniquely, the train travelled another 1,375 feet from the station down an iron pier, which led to a slope or ramp that was hinged at the other end of a platform, and which was part of a floating pontoon where the ferry itself berthed. Foot passengers could also walk the full length of the pier from the village or its proud Lincoln Castle Hotel, and cars could drive the more circuitous route round the back of the pier railway terminus and down a sloping steel ramp; a significant number were miraculously crammed onto the small car deck by a particularly positive crew. The Humber Ferry remained in service until the opening of the Humber Bridge in 1981.

Chapter 4

Moving Upmarket and Fun with 'The Riverbank boys'

In 1952, Harry Lewis sold 118 West Acridge and moved upmarket to the nearby 46 Westfield Road (referred to as Greenfield Road in Ted Lewis's first semi-autobiographical novel, *The Rabbit*, but, properly, Westfield Road). Before the move from West Acridge, Edward wrote on his bedroom wall where his signature remains today, although under modern decorations. The Victorian, three-storey, semi-detached house was resplendent with a facade of expensive, white brick on which is now affixed a Barton Civic Society commemorative plaque. Edward was again given a small back bedroom that had views over the Humber. It was adjacent to a bathroom that had its features recorded in a scene in the Ted Lewis novel *Plender*. From the house's small front garden in Westfield Road ran a passageway through to its extensive rear garden, where Edward and his friends often played wild games and that contained extensive outbuildings, including a two-storey coach house (now demolished) to the rear access of which was a small, unmade roadway leading to the parallel West Acridge. The family was now joined by the well-loved Mrs Shaw, Bertha's mother, who had moved from Stretford, and both she and the house became very dear to the young Edward as he expressed in later writings.

This well-appointed property was more appropriate to Harry's managerial status; its living room décor including not only chandeliers but a piano upon which Edward largely taught himself to play, although he was initially reluctant to demonstrate this ability. Harry, a member of the local Masonic lodge, was a tall, quiet, disciplined, firm, rather undemonstrative man, but without the commercial imperative of such erstwhile friends and neighbours as the Dickinsons and the Ashleys, who ran businesses on the then bustling Fleetgate. An example of the cross reliance of Barton's close-knit business and residential community is Horace Foster, builder of the West End Estate where the Lewises and Turners originally lived, becoming a major investor in the Ashleys' family firm, Lindsey Plumbers. Local traders and businessmen were well known to each other, with deals often being put to bed in the Conservative Club (now the Corn Exchange

Club), an imposing building presiding over Barton's Market Place, to which Harry brought his son in later life; a scenario which appeared, with poignancy, in the Ted Lewis novel *The Rabbit*.

Always known to the family as Edward, the boy was increasingly known as Lew by an established group of friends, becoming a singular character that some sought to emulate. His gang included the erstwhile West End Estate neighbours Martin and Nick Turner, John and Alan ("the Bairn") Dickinson, as well as Ted Rose, Colin Johnson, Michael Shucksmith, and Neil Ashley. Another friend at the time was Miles Hopper, who became a next-door neighbour of the Lewis family when it later downsized to 20 Westfield Road. Hopper is remembered for using a shotgun in anger towards Humber Bank birdlife, but he was later revered as a highly talented and admired wildlife painter. It was he who was portrayed as Cec in his second semi-autobiographical novel, *"driving a bread van* [which Miles did] *... the rest of the time bird-watching on the Humber Bank"*. The boys had freedom to range where they wished in their spare time. *"We crouched in a brick-littered hollow near the specked beach, temporarily out of the wind so that we could light up and smoke and talk without anything being snatched away by the elements."* The older of these boys were later to fire guns whilst National Servicemen, but Lew, who missed this requirement, portrayed the shotgun to effect in *Jack's Return Home*, remembered in the iconic pictures of a weapon-toting Michael Caine in *Get Carter*.

The new home at 46 Westfield Road gave young Lew the kudos of creating an ideal 'den': *"The narrow garden sloping away in the shadow of the tall ivy-covered barn and the gate through the orchard."* The boys converted the coach house's attic for maximum comfort; in later years installing mattresses in case any of them 'got lucky', although no one can remember if anyone did. The den was christened 'Kegsby Hall' ('kegs' being a slang word for trousers or pants). Number 46 became 'open house'. There they smoked, and talked of school, films, their other mates and girls, just hanging out (as is now the expression), and there they were often supplied liberally with cake and tea by the popular Bertha for whom her Edward could do no wrong. As Ted Lewis, he described in some writings just staring at the views around him and dreaming. Indeed, friends often recall the image of Lew, the dreamer. A bravura slogan on one Kegsby Hall wall read 'Marilyn slept here', a harmless, youthful, film-star fantasy. It was also through the back path from West Acridge that the fictitious 'Victor Graves', a thinly disguised Ted Lewis, fled his youthful pursuers in *The Rabbit* and where those youths killed one of Fred Metcalf's domestic geese in the orchard route into to number 46's garden; a gruesome discovery the next day and a real concern for Lew's friend, Nick Turner for Fred was Nick's cousin.

Taking advantage of the semi-rural River Humber countryside, Lew and his friends, later referred to as 'The Riverbank Boys', would continue to roam the great, open spaces that, in later life, became the subject of the adult Lewis's oil paintings *The Humber Bank* and *Nadine*. Life was so free they could camp at Ferriby Goss (where they frightened visiting boys in the dark with ghoulish ghost stories) and explore Bore Wood and the Rabbit Pit *"holy places to the friends I loved"*. However, their real favourite haunt was the derelict Humber Bank cement works.

Chapter 5

'The Old Cements'

It is impossible to underestimate the influence that the youngsters' outdoor adventures had on Ted Lewis's later writings, especially those in the area referred to as 'The Old Cements', a nickname given locally for the derelict Skelsey's Adamant Cement Works at Ness End on the Humber Bank, west of Barton town. Ted Lewis based scenes upon this area in no less than four of his novels.

The boys would not have fully appreciated the history of the site, but solid and advanced construction was the reason its skeleton buildings remained after the machinery was stripped out and the site abandoned in the late 1920s. George William Skelsey was a member of an entrepreneurial Yorkshire family, a scion of which began manufacturing cement at Stoneferry in Hull. Cement is made from a combination of alluvial clay, chalk and water, dried to a powder in kilns, and Skelsey discovered that such materials were also to be found in abundance on the Humber's south bank. In 1890, Skelsey's Adamant Cement Co. Ltd built its works at Ness End, manufacturing cement under the trade name of Adamant. Initially the site consisted of several of stand-alone kilns, but, later, purchasers of the successful business constructed an innovative rotary kiln on four Stonehenge-like piers, enabling production of cement twenty-four hours a day. A similar process is still the one used to this day. In Skelsey's time, a small, tram-like locomotive ran from New Cliff chalk quarry to the southwest of the Adamant site, and trundled down to the cement works, ultimately to transport lead-lined sacks of the finished product to a pier that jutted jauntily into the muddy Humber's tidal sandbank-bedevilled waters where barges and sloops were the natural transport. Ted Lewis later described the abandoned chalk quarry he had played in as a lad, thus. *"The cliff. Two huge worked-out chalk pits. Mysterious with thick foliage and tall dark sullen woodland."* Water was supplied to Skelsey's from a bore well on site, and clay supplied from an adjacent pit. The cement was distributed inland via the River Trent, which feeds into the Humber Estuary, or, internationally, via the newly constructed docks in Goole or from Hull docks across the estuary. Blue Circle Group, which purchased Adamant in 1911, then established a plant at Melton on the north bank of the Humber in

1923. Rationalisation dictated that, in 1927, Adamant production should be transferred north to the Melton plant or south to another at Melton Ross. However, de-commissioning such a series of solid buildings was clearly too expensive a task, so only the main machinery was removed, leaving an unguarded, disused melange of largely brick structures of heroic and poetic proportions; an inviting adventure landscape for future generations of Barton youth. It was to this area that those young people traditionally repaired for fun, far away from the prying eyes of adults.

In modern times, reclamation involving returning the site to nature would be required; an example of which occurred in the 1980s when Barton's redundant ACC chemical plant became Waters' Edge Country Park. Although a contaminated site, it was an area – just as many others were in earlier, less-enlightened days – that Edward had foraged for chicken feed together with his schoolmate, David Tideswell, both unaware of any inherent dangers. Likewise, in the late 1940s and early 1950s, Adamant's buildings largely remained as enticing edifices to climb on and hide in. Some of the wharf and pier remained in the 1950s, although it is largely unrecognisable now following the 2013 tidal surge. Ted Lewis, in his first novel, described them, again with intensity of feeling and nostalgia as *"The disused cement works on the river bank, overgrown and decaying, plaster peeling from the brickwork, the bricks themselves working loose and tumbling down, creating miniature screes around the roofless shells of buildings. The remains of a small pier rotting quietly through the seasons."* This quarry site is still visible.

Edward and his friends naturally took full advantage of The Old Cements, where their activities included acting out films involving gangsters or western heroes. Life was free, sometimes ferocious or daring. When twelve, Edward and his friend Nick Turner purchased Robin cigarettes in small packets or singly from Rowson's shop on Fleetgate, secreting them in a kiln hollow to smoke later. The interior of Rowson's shop can now be seen in the museum at Barton's Baysgarth House, a building that was once part of Barton Grammar School where Edward was educated. Smoking, sadly, became his lifetime lethal habit when it was more endemic; Bertha Lewis was often to be seen with a cigarette dangling from her lips, the front of her hair stained with nicotine. Nick Turner recounts not only their smoking habits but how the boys climbed the tall, brick piers on which the rotary kiln had been supported, pretending it was a drop of 100 feet on Mount Everest, which had just been conquered in 1953. *"He would always insist on being Edmund Hillary to my Sherpa Tenzing,"* describes Nick, ruefully. Another former friend maintained *"Ed* (Lew) *possibly felt he had to prove himself being younger and smaller"* and *"He tended to push himself further than the rest."*

Not only was Edward accepted by older boys, in turn he accepted younger ones such as Alan ('the Bairn') Dickinson, John's younger brother, and was not above having his leg pulled. Mike Shucksmith once took it upon himself to lampoon Lew by daubing a very rude image in white paint on one of the kiln walls. Nick Turner relates graphically, *"He labelled it 'E LEWIS'. This did not go down very well with Edward, as you can imagine, and no one really wanted to fall out with him. Mike was inventive and cleverly altered the caption to 'THE LEWISHAM COLLEGE'."*

Vivid descriptions of The Old Cements are to be found in *All the Way Home and All the Night Through* and *The Rabbit*. Yet it was in *Jack's Return Home*, renamed *Carter* and *Get Carter* after the eponymous film had gone on general distribution, that we find Ted Lewis using the area as a film location to describe its final denouement, the unexpected but inevitable grisly death of Jack Carter, *"I walked up the side of the bank and followed him watching him disappear into the overgrown brickyard ... I could hear him scrambling over miniature screes of bricks that had fallen from the decaying walls. The sound had the rattle of death." and again "On my right boundary was a long low kiln so old hat its tip was totally covered with grass ... Beyond the tileries, out of sight, were the remains of the landing stage... Frank [fictional Jack Carter's brother] and me used to sit on the edge of the vats and throw bangers in and watch them fizz across the surface of the water."* The dust jacket of *Jack's Return Home* portrays an image of criminal enforcer Jack Carter dangling a shotgun and wearing a trilby hat, which gangster Jack 'The Hat' McVitie, and others like him, wore before he was mercilessly slayed by Reggie Kray in 1967. This is an uncanny pose that is like an actual photograph of Lew posing on a kiln, albeit without a shotgun, taken by his friend Neil Ashley.

Ted Lewis's dark, revenge-based novel, *Plender*, also features The Old Cements; *"It took me two hours to drive round the river* [Humber] … *I drive on to the narrow track that wound down the lee of the Wolds towards the river and the quarry. I knew every slope, every hollow, every track. We'd come here most every weekend when we were kids. The perfect playground for the games we played. The narrow-gauge lines were still as they used to be, lazily curving away into the quarry basin … I lifted out the body and took it over to one of the panniers … the pannier toppled over back to its original position, sealing off the trench and the body."* Ted Lewis could have chosen a site on the north bank of the Humber for the character to secrete that body, but, instead, his main character drives many miles from Hull to somewhere the author knew and could describe with conviction.

Chapter 6

"Movies were Movies"

In the late 1940s and 1950s, cinemas were a principal source of entertainment countrywide, and families would often visit them twice a week, depending on budget, regardless of the film on show. It would not be unusual to take in a *Citizen Kane* or Will Hay film with a pinch of George Formby. The Lewis family was no stranger to this habit, which was later limited by the advent of television. That entertainment, now taken for granted in every home, had its debut in the 1930s, but its spread was largely halted by World War II. However, enthusiasm to view Her Majesty Queen Elizabeth II's Coronation on 2nd June 1953 was a watershed. The screening was enjoyed by around 20.4 million people who, a survey said, watched the ceremony for least half an hour. As there were only 2.7 million private television sets, public screens were given special collective-viewing licenses enabling 1.5 million people to enjoy the event in ballrooms, hospitals, churches, London's Royal Festival Hall, The Odeon in Leicester Square, and Butlin's holiday camps in resorts such as Filey, Skegness and Clacton. Television had thus arrived as the principal viewing medium. Thirteen-year-old Edward had already acquired and retained a very special interest in films, when regularly 'going to the pictures', 'the flicks' or 'the movies'.

At that time, the Lewis family did own a television, referred to in both of Ted Lewis's semi-autobiographical novels. Despite television becoming more popular, the two cinemas in Barton remained for many years the habitual places of resort for young and old alike. Edward, however, paid particular attention to acting, screenplay and the technical side of direction, an obsession that became a major influence on his later writing. This attention to the technical detail of films enabled his novels to read very much like a film script of which his purple passage describing Barton is a classic example *"A town remembered in perpetual Kodachrome"*.

Although for some years in the same ownership, there were definite distinctions between the two Barton cinemas, The Star at the corner of High Street and Holydyke, and The Oxford Picture House and Theatre of Varieties situated at the corner of Newport and Maltby Lane.

The Oxford was considered the superior. Still showing a distinctive facade, it is now disused, in disrepair and something of a blight on the area. In 1922 it had become the second cinema to be opened in the town, equipped with wooden, double seats in the balcony upstairs to accommodate the wishes of courting couples, which often included Edward. The Oxford had yet another sophistication. Whereas the old-style films required the use of a twin-spool projector, the advent of new cellular film enabled the use of only one. A projectionist required considerable skill to synchronise transference of the old spool to the following one seamlessly and pre-celluloid films could easily burst into flames from the heat. The Oxford acquired the necessary single-spool projector and could screen longer feature films without a problem. The Star, on the other hand, relied on twin-spool projection, which meant it usually screened shorter B movies or risked jagged interruptions of features at the crucial moment, to choruses of *"Why are we waiting?"*, and the embarrassment of Mr Hill, the manager, who liked to impose discipline in the house and was quite capable of throwing out difficult customers, young and old. The prices were higher at the Oxford as the atmosphere was more sophisticated, and the cinema could afford better quality films as well as screening them more effectively.

Before 1953, both cinemas were owned by Cliff Whitley, who also possessed a distinctive boat that Lew and the boys would recognise when it was often moored adjacent to the cement works. Both cinemas also had a stage, but The Oxford boasted two dressing rooms. As it was older, The Star was less comfortable than the Oxford. *"The house lights were still up and the smell of dusty carbolic was perfume in my nostrils"* Ted Lewis later wrote. The Star was given a local nickname, 'The Ranch', because of its reliance on cowboy films as B movies. In the 1950s, cinema programmes could include the main feature and a second, usually shorter, one, which became known as the 'B movie'. The term became associated with a lower budget film, but as double feature programmes later faded out, so did B movies. The cinemas in Barton had a three-day programme running twice a week, with two performances on Saturday night as well as a matinee. Both Barton cinemas feature in Ted Lewis novels, particularly in *Jack's Return Home/Get Carter*, which includes a mixture of Scunthorpe and Barton locations; *"as I got closer to the*

High Street I noticed it wasn't raining anymore. I turned left and walked up the High Street, I passed the Oxford Cinema." After Lew went to college in Hull in 1957, The Star cinema closed before it could invest in the new projection system and was demolished to make way for an innovation, the supermarket, which is now Barton's only traditional ironmonger, Fleetgate Hardware.

Barton's street scene was also significant because Edward's day and night life is woven into his two later Barton based semi-autobiographical novels. The Star was number 127 High Street, and had an adjacent house (still standing). Next to this, as described in *The Rabbit*, was 'Johnson's builders yard', in real life Thompson's Yard where Harry Lewis parked his van as there were no garages either at 118 West Acridge or 46 Westfield Road. Moving further east, you would come to a row of terraced houses, known as Winship Flags, opposite the Coach and Horses, the pub in which Lew's school friend, Zilla Yarwood, lived with her grandmother who was the licensee. Still in Barton, Zilla Gilfoy (née Yarwood) provided invaluable colour about her friend, Edward, since she went to both of his schools, and often travelled on the same Humber Ferry as him when she later went to her clerical work in Hull and he to college studies. Both Thompson's Yard and Winship Flags were demolished in the 1960s, and, after life as a car park, became part of the present Lidl store.

That area whole gave contextual relevance to Ted Lewis's Barton based novel *The Rabbit* (1975). One incident in the book relates how youths espy the fictitious Victor Graves on his way home. They seek to beat him following an incident in a pub earlier that night. Victor takes to his heels and evades them by returning home not directly down Westfield Road to his home and which would have involved passing the youths lounging on the corner but on a circuitous route along High Street area and other roads, ultimately to the West Acridge access home.

In the late 1950s and 1960s there was an American movement for B movies to focus on darker subjects, including the exploitation of vulnerable females who were often pictured in enticing poses on posters. These movies also featured horror, science fiction and faux excitement, often with fanciful plots appealing particularly to the young. There still exists a cult following for this celluloid tradition, and, had he lived, Ted Lewis would undoubtedly have numbered himself as a collector of these. He retained a fascination for this type of film all his life, particularly those starring Ernest Borgnine whose career took off in 1951. Later in life, the writer's conspicuous talent was to weave their excitement factor it into his crime fiction, whilst deftly presenting plots and characters that were rather more complex, compelling and, for the most part, credible. It is generally recognised that his favourite B movie was *Shack Out on 101*, a 1955 American noir film directed by Edward Dein, starring Ted's other hero, Lee Marvin. The plot is instructive. The war-veteran owner of a seaside diner lusts after his sexy waitress, but so does her boyfriend, a scientist customer, who works at a nearby hush-hush military base. Marvin steals the show as Slob, a short-order cook who turns out to be a spy using the diner undercover for smuggling nuclear secrets out of the country. Slob features in the opening sea-shore scenes forcing kisses on the bikini clad waitress and he is also filmed callously striking her. Edward and the lads played much of this action out at The Old Cements, and, as Ted Lewis, found ease in graphically describing such abuse. *Shack Out on 101* is a noir film, considered one of the best to come out of the American Poverty Row Studios where many B movies were made. His mother, Bertha, always maintained Edward really wanted to be another James Dean.

Such noir films emerged in the 1940s and 1950s, and were springboards for the Ted Lewis writings, particularly the crime novels. There is a glimpse of this trend in his first description of the abuse of the opposite sex as an essential part of his very first novel *All the Way Home and All the Night Through* (1965). Friends and acquaintances do not speak of Edward encountering such domestic violence in real life and there is no known history of domestic violence in his family, which indulged him as an only child. Thus, initially, Ted Lewis could write of the incomprehension and utter unreasonableness of his alter ego, Victor Graves, *"the final red of my trembling violence burned into my eyes and I hit her across the mouth ... Everything snapped back into my mind. I saw what I had done. My mouth hung open at the comprehension ... I didn't mean to hurt you ... you know I love you."* This sensitivity is absent in later crime novels where disfiguring a lady's face is treated as almost commonplace, and with increasing regularity and venom.

Later in life, Ted Lewis described in a handwritten article, subsequently published, some roots of his inspiration as *"In the days before the commonplace of TV Travel, only the cinema provided a mirror to other worlds and a pretty limited mirror at that ... Films and books provided an escape ... I create a private world in one of my own books, it's a form of escapism."*

Chapter 7

Barton Grammar School

1951 to 1956

Ted Lewis, was mainly referred to as Edward at school, often shortened to Ed. He passed the eleven plus to qualify for Barton Grammar School, then with its entrance on Caistor Road, which is to the east of and leading out of Barton to the outlying villages. He enrolled on 9th September 1951, being number nine hundred and sixty-four on the School Admissions Register. Each day he would cycle to school, often having to dodge cow droppings from cows still driven down Barton roads by Farmer Hoodless from his Humber Bank fields to his buildings on Holydyke. Edward had missed a good amount of schooling because of his rheumatic fever, but when he became interested in girls, he used this to his advantage by spinning them the impish yarn that he had nearly died, hoping and often succeeding to engender the hapless victim's sympathy. Naturally, he had also been focussed on more interesting youthful leisure activities, so it was his inherent intelligence that rewarded him. The school had been opened in 1931 to serve Barton town alone, but then the 1944 Education Act created the tripartite educational system, grammar schools for the more scholastically gifted, secondary modern schools for those who did not pass the eleven-plus examination, and secondary technical schools for those seeking technical qualifications. These and other demographic changes had an ultimate effect on how secondary education worked for Edward. Under tertiary education, which lasted until effectively abolished by the 1975 Education Act in favour of comprehensive education, Barton's pupils attended either Beretun Secondary Modern School on Barrow Road or Barton Grammar School. Outlying areas, such as Immingham, had no grammar school, so pupils there who had passed their eleven plus were also in the catchment area of Barton Grammar School, and accordingly swelled the numbers at Barton Grammar School beyond the capacity of its original building.

Edward and his family knew the Georgian Baysgarth House with its Victorian additions, and Baysgarth Park as an integral part of the town, and the park was a well-used leisure area. These had been gifted by the then owner to Barton Urban District Council in 1930. Faced with a need to educate Immingham pupils, the house was deemed a suitable overflow for. Barton Grammar School, so it was designated to accommodate fourth-, fifth- and sixth-form pupils. When Edward started school in 1951, aged eleven, the first form was divided into two streams, L and M; he was placed in M, which was designated for pupils who were more practical. Edward was incensed at what he regarded as a slight on his intelligence. Although *"in reality the main difference was that the L stream learned Latin as they only had one teacher of that subject!"* remembers Nick Turner, who was in the same year, but in the L stream. Other friends at the school included John Dickinson and Neil Ashley. Edward had developed an independent streak and was far from a star pupil; a natural rebel. He has been described as having a kind of stubborn toughness in the classroom. He continued to be a cheeky chappie and was popular with most of his peers. Norman Goddard had been appointed headmaster at around the same time as Edward started at the grammar school, an appointment that was viewed with trepidation by many staff because Goddard, although a musician of repute with strong organisational skills, was well known as a very strict disciplinarian. True to form, his long career at Barton Grammar School was peppered with anecdotes of pouncing on even minor pupil transgressions and meting out what he perceived was an appropriate punishment, but which we might question today. It was not long before Edward Lewis fell afoul of Goddard on a regular basis and it was apparent that Goddard, who expected upright deportment, an alert attitude and respectful conduct, often picked on the boy. These were anathema to Edward whose irreverent conduct was renowned. The boy was frequently in trouble for transgressions, but the clash came to a head when Goddard found Lewis lounging against a wall in the changing room. Edward was manhandled by Goddard and, no doubt because he was not contrite, received a hard slap on the face from Goddard. Unused to such treatment, the still-frail young boy wet himself. Ted Lewis, the author, over twenty years later, had the courage to write about such an experience in The Rabbit, although in a different context, as he recounts *"the memory of the Headmaster slapping my face and the rush of piss shattering on to the classroom floor, uncontrollable because of my illness-weakened bladder."* Although Goddard was an unbending classical musician, Edward, whose interest in jazz was growing, might have been surprised that the headmaster was spotted by fellow pupil, Dave Mouncey, playing piano jazz when he thought no one else was about.

After his return to Barton in 1974 as Ted Lewis, he recounted meeting his former headmaster Goddard when both were travelling to Hull on the Humber Ferry. Goddard recognised the novelist and complimented him on having made good in the end. A put-down quick-to-the-lips barb from Jack Carter would have been called for, but at the time Ted Lewis was in a bad place, both emotionally and financially, and did not relate any triumphant riposte. Indeed, there had been a time when Edward had acquired a photograph of Goddard and framed it in a toilet seat, an escapade he remembered with glee and recounted to others in later life. Whilst Edward would habitually sit quietly at the back of his classroom, often next to Dave Mouncey, there is no doubt that Edward pushed the boundaries of school tolerance as far as he could. He would sketch on the blackboard during the break time until caught one day. One example was flouting a rule that, when walking from the main school building on Caistor Road to Baysgarth House, pupils could not cross the corner of the garden of the private house adjacent to Baysgarth Park. Edward regularly ignored this, for which he was regularly given one hundred lines. Another notorious occasion occurred when an exasperated new mistress gave Edward two thousand lines, but the boy was not fazed, and would not let a perceived injustice rest until he had argued his case and limited the punishment to only a few hundred. The legendary Edward, later adult Ted Lewis, was charm in action, pushing risky boundaries to the limit.

Edward did join the music group and performed in school plays, where he found respect for the master, Ray Smithson, later the first head of Baysgarth Comprehensive when tertiary education ended in 1975. Smithson, whose life interest was in music and drama, also took pupils, including Edward, on school trips abroad, most notably a 1955 ten-day walking holiday in Luxemburg. It was no coincidence that, when writing his first novel, the kindly and perceptive head of the Art College in Hull was named Smithson; *"I knew from experience that he was an honest man, concerned with his own work and with the work of the students ... He gave me a smile full of relieved earnest satisfaction."* Edward was also cast as Donaldbain and as a soldier in Henry Treece's production of Macbeth, in which his friends, John

Dickinson and Mike Shucksmith, also appeared. Richard (Dick) Scott, who was in years above Edward, remembers his friend selecting short two- or three-character plays: *"These would be learned and directed by Edward and performed at 46 Westfield Road where I often played piano for the necessary introduction or accompaniment as I had received instruction and Edward was performing."*

Although, as Victor Graves, Ted Lewis described schooldays as "suffocating", he did achieve a Special Art Prize after his second year and a General Proficiency Prize in his School Certificate year. He was also always an observer of those whom he met. Keith Phillips, whose nickname was 'Glegger', was a tough youth at the grammar school and was later characterised as the rough, assured, tough, teddy-boy quarry worker, Clacker, who unmercifully picks on Victor Graves in *The Rabbit*. That colourful schoolboy gripped Edward's imagination and he later appears later in *Plender* when there is a reprise of boys' exploration of their pubescent sexuality: *"Bet you can't fetch." "I can,"* said Peter, *"I can shoot 3 feet. Even Glegger in 4M can't shoot that far."*

Under the influence of Henry Treece, however, Edward excelled in essays; his contributions to *The Bartonian*, which was then the magazine of Barton Grammar School, being 'Inside Information' in 1954 when he was fourteen, 'The Legend' in 1955 when he was fifteen, and 'Double Shuffle' in 1956, the year in which he left the school. 'Inside Information' is the story of a Local Authority employee who comes to remove an old man from his derelict home, only to find it was in that same room, his own grandfather had murdered the old man's grandfather. The occupant takes revenge by beating the Local Authority man to death with the same poker. 'Double Shuffle' describes, in an uncanny and knowing way, the adverse effects of drinking. The writer turns out to be a mental patient who must be returned to a mental hospital. The sub plot is that he had lost his and his mother's money gambling and drinking in the city on a trip from the countryside where he was brought up; *"He boarded the train in Salt Flats City, alone. When he arrived in the City he found himself alone ... Aloneness surging round him from the neon lights."* In his attempt to convey the feeling of loneliness, Lewis fell into the easy trap of not only unnecessarily and unwittingly repeating words but not editing his piece sufficiently, errors he did not make in later life.

Three things are particularly striking: the degree to which the boy deals with the worldly experience that drink yields false bonhomie, his undisclosed loneliness and his sense of the macabre. Edward's friends also contributed to *The Bartonian*. John Dickinson's subject was appropriately medical as he later trained for that profession and the article of Neil Ashley, who wrote insightfully about the benefit in harnessing technical developments, was a herald to his later successful life in engineering and business. Parents of both friends owned businesses in the town, so also contributed to the magazine by placing advertisements extolling the benefit of their firms' services. Edward's short story 'Double Shuffle' opens with a man arriving in the town on a train and immediately repairing to a pub, identical to the opening in the most famous Ted Lewis novel, *Jack's Return Home.*

Edward left the grammar school at sixteen to return for one re-union in later life. Old boys felt that they were honoured to have a significant artist as one of the scholars. Baysgarth House is now a museum leased by North Lincolnshire Council to the charity CHAMP Ltd, which, despite representation, has unaccountably not seen fit to give recognition to the history and life of Ted Lewis in the very place he studied. The importance of Barton's novelist has, however, been recognised by its Civic Society, which holds seventeen of Ted Lewis's 1979 sketches. The Wilderspin National School Heritage Museum on Queen Street, Barton in partnership with both the Civic Society and the Ted Lewis Group have accepted the challenge to preserve the local heritage of the town's local artist

Edward Lewis might have been destined for clerical work or to follow his father into an artisan style of lower management, but for the foresight of Barton Grammar School's Head of English, Henry Treece.

Chapter 8

Henry Treece
1911 to 1966

Henry Treece, Head of English at Barton Grammar School, was loved by all and, in his own distinctive way, charismatic. Recognition by Treece of his pupil's talents was a major influence on Ted Lewis's writing career. Treece had not always been a teacher and, as such, there are many parallels with the American action-man novelist, Ernest Hemingway (1899–1961). Henry Treece was born twelve years after Hemingway and died in 1966, five years later than Hemingway. Treece suffered, as Edward did, with severe childhood health problems; in Treece's case, meningitis and pneumonia. He went on to defeat those problems, becoming a powerful man at university, playing hockey and captaining the university boxing team. Hemmingway's wife's birthday present to her husband in Key West was a boxing ring. Treece, like young Edward, loved sketching, having also been treated to a myriad of pictures in childhood. Like Edward, Treece played piano, especially the blues, to an acceptable dance-band standard. Treece was also a composer, and Fletcher DuBois, biographer of 1960s iconic folk singer Joan Baez, recounts that the winsome artist recorded five of Treece's songs. Edward had a piano at home and, although he was given some lessons, was mostly self-taught; however, he had advice from and an example in Henry Treece, and, probably later, pianist and organist, Harold Johnson. In 1937, Treece was in Santander receiving a degree in Spanish; the same year Hemingway was in Spain, sometimes living in Madrid, whilst reporting on the Civil War. Treece, therefore, had adventure in his bones and so did his pupil, Edward Lewis.

Henry Treece, critic, musician, writer and poet, had considerable stature in the literary world and could not have been a better example for Edward Lewis whom he advised and tutored with care. It was said that Ted Lewis's manuscripts, which initially he wrote into exercise books, needed little editing, and this is likely to be attributable to his early instruction. In 1938, Treece had met Dylan Thomas, and had followed him round America in later years; they later fell out when Treece wrote a criticism of the apocalyptic poetic principles propounded by Thomas, but rumour has it that there was also a domestic element to the split. Dylan Thomas, died aged thirty-nine in 1953, having been admitted to hospital with alcohol-induced brain damage; a wasted talent flowing from a similar lifestyle adopted by the adult Ted Lewis, who died at just forty-two. Despite Thomas's opprobrium, Treece remained highly regarded as a literary critic, and was therefore able to hone Edward's incipient writing skills whilst not inhibiting the boy's individual skill.

It was after marrying Mary in 1939 that Treece took up his position as teacher of English at Barton Grammar School – a fortunate selection for Edward. Treece remained there all his working life apart from service as a Flight-Lieutenant in the Volunteer Reserve of the RAF. On his return to Barton, Treece was elevated to head of English, initially living on Ferriby Road in the town, but later in the then imposing East Acridge House where he died in 1966. The property backed onto the centre of Barton's ancient Saxon settlement, and Treece had a huge love and understanding of this period. Conveying his enthusiasm to young children in one of his many published works and lectures, Treece carried his ability to grip children's attention to the end. His last lecture to young people in May 1966 was described in the following terms *"He started off by telling the audience why he would like to have been a Viking* [who, of course, harried the Saxons in Barton] ... *They were spellbound because he spoke with great conviction and enthusiasm and a total lack of condescension."* In 1952, Treece published his last poetry volume, *The Exiles*, confining the rest of his artistic output to prose by writing many novels and short stories. His first novel was *The Dark Island*, which saw the light of day in 1952, and thereafter he was published on fifty-two occasions – a prodigious artistic record.

Dressed distinctively, but always with his gown over his other apparel, the popular teacher not only gripped the attention of his pupils but he had a special regard for those with whom he had a rapport. He could, as an ex-serviceman, also deal out swift physical admonition for a pupil's transgression. Writer and another former Barton Grammar pupil, Barbara Hughes, penned an article for *Lincolnshire Life* in which she recounts Treece's incisive encouragement to her as well as Edward, telling of Treece giving her his trademark conspiratorial wink of a kind reserved for special pupils. A superb raconteur, Treece was every inch a teacher for whom pupils wished to do well, hence his talents were rewarded with pupils obtaining top GCE grades; he reputedly had the best pupil exam results in the county. Nick Turner remembers Treece once inadvertently falling asleep in one lesson at Baysgarth House, unsurprising since the master was well known for working late into the night, meticulously annotating his notes and literature, as well as engaging in music and enjoying drama. Pupils understood, and simply carried on with their work for forty-five minutes and courteously woke him up when the bell rang. *"I ask only that my novels entertain,"* said Treece, which was certainly a lesson he taught Edward. After all, he understood that propensity having published a novel, The Rebels, in 1953. Treece also was admirer of Raymond Chandler's American hard-boiled novels featuring detective Philip Marlowe, which had sold in their hundreds of thousands. Treece would often read aloud from Chandler's books in an American accent. Treece's eclectic interest in such literature was worlds apart from his more prosaic writings, especially his earlier romantic poetry, of which the following is a typical example:

"And let us walk in the wood, love
Walk in the stillness of pines
And sigh for the wild birds who cry there
All night in their shuddering dreams."

One of Edward's friends, Neil Ashley, remembers with affection the happy and convivial times when pupils, particularly those in the sixth form, would be invited by Treece to his East Acridge House home, finding convivial both the teacher and his wife, Mary, who was an intriguing painter and who, it was rumoured, could appear carelessly robed on occasions – an intriguing attraction for teenage boys. Henry was pleased to be a signal mentor to Edward, and it may be the case that, but for Henry Treece, Edward might not have become as successful an author; an opinion confirmed by his now sadly deceased friend, Colin Johnson.

Treece's early novels were published by the Bodley Head having been introduced to this house by one John Johnson who went on to form the John Johnson Agency in 1956. When, as Ted Lewis, Edward finished his first novel. *All the Way Home and All the Night Through*, he needed a literary agent. The very well respected John Johnson was proposed and indeed, managed to place that first book with a publisher. Treece was a novelist, artist and musician, the pedagogue who reinforced those same capabilities in his pupil. However, it was plain to Treece that his pupil's talents were not only for English but for sketching, a skill he felt would be useful in the search for a suitable adult occupation.

Chapter 9

And Relax

Lew, as he was later popularly known, continued with his compulsion to sketch, and attended to this with focus and application, often asking sitters to remain still for significant periods with the result that some of his work was truly stunning. Then, as in later life, he would draw uncanny likenesses of his subjects and then sometimes give them away; they were to be treasured by recipients later in life.

Strict father, Harry, remained a tall, quiet, confident member of the local Masons' lodge; a sport-orientated man of his time who was particularly adept at cricket. Secure in his position then as quarry manager at Melton Ross, intriguingly his son, fictitiously as Victor Graves, regards him as sometimes weak: *"'Now, now,' my father said, embarrassed, looking from face to face with a grin that was supposed to explain away my reaction springing from youth. 'Now, now it wasn't meant the way you took it, Victor.' This was worse, the deliberate underlying of something he should have taken a stand against."* Weakness was a trait that Ted Lewis made clear in *Jack's Return Home* was to be despised; in this novel, he portrayed Jack's own brother failing to defend him, which was an event that caused a rift between them and was later avenged by Jack in the seduction of the brother's new wife just because he could. Ted Lewis's novels often portray contempt for weakness as regularly as casual sexual conquest occurring just for the challenge, not even a thrill.

Lew developed a real way with the girls; a talent that was to follow him throughout his life. Zilla Gilfoy, careful to point out that she did not succumb, explains how, when still Zilla Yarwood, she saw many girls experience the one come-hither look that could make a girl feel very special. She said, *"He was very charming and wonderful."* If you were a smoker, then all the better, for Lew was entrenched in a lifelong habit, dating from buying those Robin cigarettes when he was a twelve-year-old. As an example, legend had it that one of Lew's 'girls' was Doreen Semperingham, a fellow committed smoker, who was particularly favoured as a companion because of her habit. Lew had, with others, to achieve experience and build up his confidence. Ted Lewis shamelessly as the fictitious Victor Graves, described some very raw early sexual bravado: *"In Plaskitt's coal yard ... Jackson's bare bottom, moonlit against the black coal sacks, was rising and falling ... completing what he'd done earlier."* Fictitious early experience? If all else failed, his chat up account of nearly dying in early age could soften many a female heart.

There is no recorded account of any religious activity in the Lewis family. Barton boasted St Augustine's Roman Catholic Church, the imposing Trinity Methodist Church with its perpendicular height designed to accommodate flocks from over fourteen outlying chapels, the cosy United Reform Chapel five minutes' walk from the family home, as well as St Mary's Parish Church that nodded to St Peter's across Barton Beck, an area that, in later life, Lew sketched so skilfully. No one remembers any Lewis family attendance at these places of worship. Similarly, the characters in Ted Lewis's novels have little moral compass or spirituality, merely a sardonic view on life at best. However, Ted did have an incipient musician's youthful joy in joining in with Salvation Army hymns – an organisation significantly prepared to borrow tunes from the devil! Only at the very end of his life was Ted Lewis to seek a spiritual meaning to his life.

Although he was very much a youth of the late 1950s, Lewis was never a 'Ted' ('Teddy Boy') nor part of mainstream Barton youth *"protesting its dissatisfaction"*, as he described many contemporaries in his first novel. Accordingly, descriptions of drapes, crepes or 'DA' haircuts (named for giving the appearance of a mallard duck's arse) do not rock 'n' roll substantially through his two semi-autobiographical novels. Instead, such costumed youths usually feature as objects of antagonism. Lew, though brave, was known sometimes to have been an occasional victim of those fitter or more ruthless than himself, and who were later reflected in his fiction.

Lew was a slender youth, later nicknamed *"Thinstuff"* by fictitious Harry (Ron Burnett) in later art college days and despite being characterised as *"Fatstuff"* exclaims, *"We were all thin then."* As a teenager, Lew was significantly good looking, if rather frail from his early years as an invalid. His blonde hair developed a signature quiff, and he was usually smartly dressed in sports attire, according to Nick Turner. He was well-known locally as having an artistic bent and therefore, in his early teens, something of a target of rougher peers who thought that this was an indication of the effeminate. Much of the antagonism towards Victor Graves in *The Rabbit* is focussed on that kind of bullying.

Lew and his friends soon started drinking beer, and by fifteen were habitual drinkers in a pub-orientated society that was more relaxed and happy to turn a blind eye to this licensing transgression. It was inescapable that the group of grammar school lads imbibing in the Volunteer Arms were under eighteen, but this was accepted. As a fictional Victor Graves, he was clearly seen by his parents to have drunk to excess from time to time. Teenage youth, including Lew, would also attend dances with a view to later liaisons with compliant girls. At the Drill Hall (no longer standing) on Butts Road, an imposing 77 anti-aircraft gun was hidden at the back to enlarge the dance floor where the Harold Johnson Band entertained on a regular basis. Harold, a talented pianist, was also mentioned by Ted Lewis in *The Rabbit* as playing at the Blue Bell (now flats): *"'We've started drifting down to the Blue Bell on a Thursday these days ... Harold Johnson's been getting in there playing a bit' Mart said. 'It's not Teddy Wilson but it makes a change.'"* The Assembly Rooms was another popular venue, but the best sprung dance floor was to be found on the first floor of the imposing Town Centre Oddfellows' Hall at the corner of High Street and Queen Street.

References to Lew and his friends' appreciation of jazz greats is a feature of the autobiographical books. Victor Graves is described as noodling on the piano at home, but it is by no means clear how Lew came to treat the piano as his favourite instrument and no one can remember early tuition. Dick Scott, who had received lessons, thinks that Lew was bright enough to have taught himself. Harold Johnson's daughter, Anne, tells of Ted Lewis taking lessons from her father, but that was when the writer returned to Barton after 1974. Since those lessons could only have been to brush up on an existing skill, and he turned to Harold for this purpose, it is likely that Ted was taught either formally or informally to play in a syncopated style by that bandleader in his earlier life. Certainly, in later times, Ted Lewis had improved on his earlier inexperience and was, as Barton musician, Diane Cardee, attests, *"a really great piano player who enjoyed duets and composition."*

A flavour of the times in Barton pubs is given by Lila Harrison, now sadly no longer with us. She is distinctively identified in *The Rabbit* as a fount of all pub gossip: *"I was going to an all-night party the next day, but when I looked in the Bar, Lila told me they'd all been in, and he'd all had a good night, at least she assumed they had ... So, after Lila's news all that remained was for me to go home too."* A contemporary of Lew, her first teenage drink was in the Blue Bell at the corner of Whitecross Street and the main road through Barton, not an inconspicuous place to start under-age drinking. She and a friend went into the pub aged fifteen and, not knowing what to drink, ordered a cider. The landlord, no doubt with mischief in mind, told the girls that if they could drink the first glass, the second was on the house. The incentive was sufficient, but the consequence dire. She did not make the 100 yards or so to her house in nearby Priestgate until she staggered there much later in the evening. Later, having turned sixteen, she was enjoying a quiet drink in the Red Lion on Junction Square when the landlord, Bob Walton, announced he had to go out and asked her to mind the bar! She worked as barmaid there for some years, a concession by Bob to her youth was being allowed to knock off half an hour earlier on a Saturday night to attend dances at the Oddfellows' Hall, since this was the premier venue, and not to be missed.

Lila Harrison was a lifelong friend throughout Ted Lewis' days in Barton, although she did leave for a spell to stay in Liverpool, where she was married, and, of course, Ted left for fifteen years too. After her years at the Red Lion, Lila became a barmaid serving the upper room at The George, where music was played and that was a haunt of Lew and his friends. They were served so long as they behaved themselves. In later years, Lila ruled in the eponymous Lila's Bar, two actual saloons supervised by her from one horseshoe shaped servery.

Lew's capacity for beer from an early age was a literal taste of things to come when he started drinking himself incapable at college in Hull. The habit of youth, drinking during the first part of the evening and fighting when the mood took them, outside the Drill Hall or the Market Place, was continued later as de rigeur from the 1960s to the 1980s. In the White Lion on the Market Place, underage drinkers were 'advised' to use an upper room. Ted wrote *"Saturday night, I sat in the small room of the White Lion ... the small room was empty apart from myself."* The Volunteer Arms and Molly's Back Room were the habitual watering holes of the grammar school boys. One lunch time, recounts Dave Mouncey, grammar school master Jack Baker came into the snug at the Wheatsheaf where pupils Mouncey, Dave Patchett, Archie Campbell and others were refreshing themselves. The teacher ordered half a pint of beer himself, drank it and before he left simply commented that he did not expect to see the pupils in there again. No disciplinary action was taken, a blind eye and a gypsy's warning were considered adequate. It was believed that most of the male staff of the grammar school had served in the RAF during the war and, despite having to exert discipline, understood youths who were pushing out the boundaries with bravado.

Whatever distraction there might be, none prevented Lewis from storing up observations, later to appear as brief but stark, laconic, sardonic commentaries on people's lives, their locations or motivations. Lewis's friends increasingly began to realise that this doodling, literary, film-buff musician had developed special talents that were, even then, quite remarkable, with a personality to match.

Lew also explored wider Lincolnshire, including Scunthorpe, enabling crime novel Jack's Return Home to accurately describe Scunthorpe, GBH to take place in Mablethorpe, and have Jack Carter recognise a Grimsby accent in *Jack Carter's Law* and *Jack Carter and the Mafia Pigeon.*

Edward Lewis aged eight (centre, front row) at Barton County Primary School.

46 Westfield Road, Barton, the Lewis family home from 1952.

Original stone at Barton County Primary School, now Castledyke School.

The Humber Bank from a painting by Ted Lewis in 1964.

Interior of the Oxford Cinema, Barton.

The Star Cinema, Barton.

Barton Grammar School Photograph 1954;
Ted Lewis in top row, middle.

Barton Grammar School, now demolished.

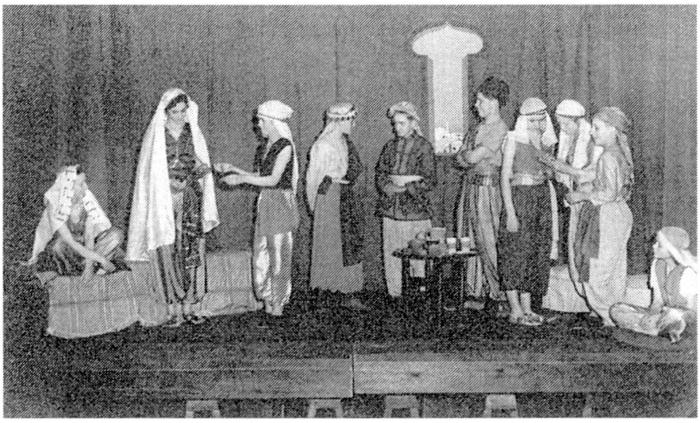

Edward in Barton Grammar School play in 1952;
Ted Lewis is fifth from left.

Henry Treece,
Head of English at
Barton Grammar
School.

Rowley's shop on Fleetgate where the boys
purchased single cigarettes.

The White Lion, Barton, featured
in *The Rabbit*, now a shop.

Ted Lewis on one of the kiln buildings at The Old Cements.

Dust cover of *Jack's Return Home* with Jack Carter sitting on a kiln.

Sand banked, Edward on the left, at Butlins Filey in 1954.

The pebbly beach at The Old Cements where there was once a jetty for transport.

Disused kilns at The Old Cements.

Kegsby Hall den at 46 Westfield Road; right to left:
Edward, Mike Shucksmith, Martin Turner, n.k.

Fleetgate with workmen waiting at the railway station (right).

Humber Ferry, *Tattershall Castle*.

Zilla Yarwood (white coat), schoolfriend of Ed Lewis, who travelled with him to Hull where she worked. Note the lack of litter and traffic in 1957.

Hull College of Arts and Crafts, now School of Performing Arts in Anlaby Road, Hull.

Stairway at Hull College of Arts and Crafts where Victor Graves in *All the Day Long and All the Night Through* fell down, when drunk, landing at the feet of the Lord Mayor.

The Unity Jazz Band. Oil Painting by Ted Lewis. Standing left to right: Ron Burnett, Tony Peacock and Tony Dugdale. Paul Richardson on the drums (rear) and Ted Lewis to the right.

Unity Jazz Band players, Lew at the rear.

The Criterion and Tower Cinemas in Hull, which Ted Lewis visited weekly.

Ted's twenty-first birthday. Right to left: Harry Lewis, Ted Lewis and Bertha Lewis.

Nick Turner when aged twenty-one.

Ted Lewis's novel about college days.

Chapter 10

Hull College of Arts and Crafts

Graphics, Art, Music, Ladies of the Day and Night

1956 to 1960

Lew, for this is how he was also known at college, was at a crossroads as he left school at sixteen. It was Henry Treece who had not only recognised Lew's literary bent but also that the young man's artistic skills should form the basis of further education in graphic art, an area which could well provide his pupil with a good living. The Lewis family would normally have expected their son to either follow his father or pursue another practical career. Lew's friend John Dickinson had long espoused an ambition towards medicine. That kind of ambition was by no means universal for, as in the description of Barton in *All the Way Home and All the Night Through* records, most people did not then leave their home town for work. Henry Treece enthused Lew with the suggestion that he pursue further education, and spoke to Lew's parents about a possible course for their son at Hull College of Arts and Crafts. In *The Rabbit*, Lewis suggests that there was some resistance from Victor's father to the proposal and that his father indicated he would have preferred his son to pursue a career more akin to his own. There is no real evidence from contemporaries of any such objection in Lew's real life; a better view being that his parents were proud of their son's talents and were prepared to invest in them. Indeed, friend Nick Turner, who had known the family since their West Acridge days, feels they were always very indulgent to their only son and, in a subsequent passage in *The Rabbit*, Harry is seen to be encouraging his son to keep up his holiday sketching.

Accordingly, in late 1956, Ted Lewis enrolled in an illustration and graphic design course at the Hull College of Arts and Crafts. Its imposing, double-fronted, Victorian building was purpose built in 1905; its design the subject of an architectural competition. In the entrance hall is an imposing cantilever staircase leading to classrooms in which life classes, architectural and graphic work, and fine art could be taught and practised. There was a large assembly hall in which regular dances took place on Saturday nights. In 1962, the year after Ted graduated, the college was renamed as the Hull College of Art and Design, and moved to new premises in Queens Gardens in

1972. It is now, rather sadly, hidden behind trees, but alive inside as the School of Performing Arts. A contemporary alumnus was David Remfry RA, two years younger than Ted and a student in a different department, who went on to have his first one-man show at Hull's Ferens Art Gallery, and achieved national and local recognition for his figurative watercolour paintings. However, both had an immediacy of intuitive characterisation in their line drawing. As Ted Lewis, he did return to fine art when he was living in Sussex between 1971 and 1974, painting watercolours and holding an exhibition with a local artist, John Westleve, who lived in a cottage nearby to which Ted would often repair after running out of cigarettes – an excuse for running out of the house.

In the early days, Lew travelled each weekday by train from Barton Railway Station to the former railway village of New Holland, which was at the shortest convenient place on the Humber Bank for a crossing to Hull. A direct ferry crossing had been inaugurated in 1820 from Hull to New Holland by *PS Magna Carta*, this vessel's name being commemorated in the name of the only existing pub now open in the village. Railway ownership of the ferry dates from 1845, and after Britain's railways were amalgamated into major regional groupings in 1923, the service, unusually, came under the control of the London & North Eastern Railway Co. (LNER) so the journey by rail and ferry was seamless.

Lew used the Humber ferries Lincoln Castle, Wingfield Castle, Tattershall Castle or Farringford for a journey that was twenty minutes long provided it successfully dodged the notorious sandbanks in the tidal, silted, fickle, muddy Humber Estuary. If the craft occasionally ground to a halt on one of the mud banks it could arrive at Hull's pier head up to an hour late or, at worst, would need to wait until the tide floated the ferry off. Ted Lewis writes *"I walked on the car deck and leant against the ferry's side and watched the last passengers cross the gangplank. Then two of the ferry's crew pulled the chains on the gangplank's pulleys and the gangplank rattled to its vertical position. The paddlewheels began to turn and the ferry drifted swiftly away from the shadow of the pontoon, out into the sunlight breadth of the river ... the ferry thumped across the river ... sidled into the landing stage at Hull Pier ... The ferry and the pontoon bumped together and the paddles back-peddled ... the passengers collected in a semicircle on the perimeter of the drawbridge's arc and two of the crew trundled open the iron gates and the drawbridge began to fall. Then came the final crash and the passengers funnelled forward."*

Ted Lewis wrote acute, accurate descriptions of the pier head (Victoria/ Corporation Pier) where, as Victor Graves, he had 'fictitious' trysts or farewells from relationship breakups, which are the focus of his two locally based novels: *"It was like a film set ... lap, lap went the river ... The buildings themselves were brooding, unhappy remains of other days. They grudgingly housed ticket office and customs authority, waiting-room and haulage business, warehouse and café. In the middle of the street (or rather square) stood a low and narrow public convenience. Standing on its own, on my immediate left, was a pub, its presence creating a narrow street between itself and the other block."* After his ferry journey, it was a ten-minute walk past the litter- and produce-strewn wholesale Fruit Market, along Hull's down-at-heel, cobbled, dockside streets, through rows of modern shops still recovering from war to arrive at the Arts College on Anlaby Road (in semi-autobiographical novels he called it Allenby Road).

The author reminds us that when he was in Hull, trolley buses and trams still ran, giving readers a flavour of Hull as a busy port, but only glimpses of its intricately built, often imposing, seventeenth- and eighteenth-century commercial centre or the city's often still-cobbled Old Town streets, yearning to be regenerated. Descriptions in the first novel are often confined to the places where he and other students met, and jazz gigs took place. In less salubrious corners of Hull, a seaman or fisherman could still come ashore and, given the paucity of late night entertainment, might buy bottles of whisky under the counters of known cafés, or perhaps be 'entertained' by a 'lady' who might easily be found in The Earl de Gray and other known hostelries. Ted Lewis does, however, occasionally describe such places such as in the following passage from his Hull based first Novel: *"The Albert Hall. Dockers' pub. Pro's pub. Licensed for singing in the huge upstairs room. Rough pub ... Victorian pub. Drinking pub. Dedicated to drinking. Powder blue gabardine suit pub, double-breasted ... twenty-inch bottoms white open-necked shirt pub. Hard pub."*

For four years, until 1960, Lew honed his graphic art, also achieving a reputation as a likely lad. To begin with he travelled from Barton, then later lived in digs, but with his father's financial support, in a bedsit down Ash Grove, which is a mile and a half from the college, straight down the main road north out of Hull in the direction of Beverley. His alter ego, Victor Graves, in *All the Way Home and All the Night Through* and *The Rabbit*, found contact with his Barton friends became stretched, especially with John Dickinson (Philip in fiction), who soon left Barton to study medicine in London. As a student, Lew was saving up experiences so he could include them in his first novel, which Judy Burnett (Jenny in the novel) maintains *"reads like a diary of event they all shared."*

Lew continued to make friends easily. He was interesting and approachable with male friends and acquaintances, and a magnet for the girls. Although he still retained a calculated cool and disinterested air, designed to inject an air of mystery, his capacity to enchant and often exploit the opposite sex was legendary. As one of his contemporary students, Roger Sharpless recalls with humour, *"He had a real reputation. You only had to open a store cupboard door to find Lew fall out with Janet Camm."* He also combed his hair in a signature quiff, anticipating the appearance pop idol Billy Fury adopted to make girls swoon. Lew was also generous in finding girls for his male friends. On one occasion, John Dickinson was invited to one of the college dances but had no partner, so Lew readily agreed supply one. To John's great consternation, on first meeting in a local pub, the date pulled out a pipe and started to smoke it. Ted had a genuinely kind disposition. Barry Atkinson remembers that, as a new student, he was sent out on a bitterly cold outdoor project, *"I came back to the college from Pearson's Creek, nithered. Ted Lewis was in the foyer – obviously well-known and popular, talking with friends. Seeing how new and cold I was, he came over to me, looked at my work with interest and made me feel welcome. I'll never forget that."* Many students of that era remember Ted, with his assured, welcoming air and good looks, with great affection – even those not in his close circle of friends, who were fiercely loyal to him.

Lew's recreations were frequent visits to the cinema, drinking, girls and, later, playing jazz; the latter providing opportunities to enjoy the previous two. He could exploit these experiences in drawing word pictures of many characters he observed in life. His talent in observation was akin to the ability of fine-art student David Remfry, of whom Michael Hearn related in 2012 that it was at Hull's Locarno dance hall where Remfry began his best-known series of paintings. Said Remfry, *"There is no better way to express this through sketching in dance halls. They were kind of dodgy, a little bit risky. Hull had a big fishing industry so you got the young guys off the trawlers. They carried open razors. These Northern Teddy Boys may have dressed in well-tailored suits but they were dangerous. And it's difficult – you don't want to draw attention to yourself."* Lew retained a similar capacity of all his life, for even in the days in Barton at the end of his short life, fellow drinkers and other friends describe a quite unassuming man sitting back quietly with his drink observing all that was going on.

By comparison, Ted Lewis's quality of observation is illustrated when he wrote of Victor Graves one night going to the College dance *"There is group of figures on the steps below me ... passing the bottle around ... the yobs who tried to get into the dance. One says 'Hey up lads. One of the Mr bleedin' clever students.' I draw level with him and he pushes me viciously in the chest ... His face twists with quick hatred ... His hands go to my face and a fist belonging to somebody clangs me on the side of my head knocking me off my feet ... I feel the boots go in."* It was fancy dress that night and Victor (also in real time, Lew) wore a full cowboy outfit, but had lost his hat. He was smashed with alcohol and the worse for wear from the fists of others. Ted Lewis described his alter ego staggering from the top of those magnificent college stairs, bringing pictures down in an uncontrolled descent finding that *"At the bottom of the stair the Mayor and his wife and the Sheriff and the Sheriff's lady and the Principal of the College and head of the Painting Department are about to enter the Hall to judge the fancy dress competition."*

Friend Nick Turner recalls a Remfry-like observation when the two friends were in the Humber Ferry saloon when a group of trawlermen tumbled through in a cloud of expletives, demanding copious outlandish beverages, 'three-day millionaires' playing poker for real money. Ted was transfixed. He lapped up every obscene word, each savage taunt, and their capacity to drink and roar simultaneously. Nick describing, *"As he picked up something they dropped from the table and returned it to the swaying group it was as if Ted was totally obsequious to the image before us."* After his time at Hull

College, Remfry had a passing acquaintance in Earls Court with artist Francis Bacon and so did Ted Lewis, but for him it was at the infamous drinking den, the Colony Club on Dean Street, Soho. Remfry later lived in the iconic Chelsea Hotel in New York, absorbing its unique atmosphere enjoyed by the likes of Jack Kerouac, Janis Joplin and Dylan Thomas, the latter with whom Ted Lewis had the parallel distinction of ultimately drinking himself to death. Lew would have loved the ambiance of the hotel and been envious of Remfry's experiences.

Lew's days often merged into nights; unsurprisingly, as he would often visit cinemas for hours, up to three days a week, to satisfy his fascination with film. Next door to the art college was Anlaby Road's Tower Cinema, directly opposite stood the Regent, and on the main junction with Carr Lane was the plusher Cecil Cinema. The Criterion, the Curzon (known for its foreign movies) and the Dorchester all fronted George Street, less than a ten-minute walk from the college. The Carlton was half a mile further up Anlaby Road. The ABC, which later hosted The Beatles live (for a fee of £850 in 1963) in its heyday, was but two minutes away. Sadly, none of these, which were, to Lew, blissful palaces of fantasy, have survived as cinemas. He was no longer confined to Barton's 'Ranch' or the 'B Movie Corral', becoming even more steeped in celluloid, and enhancing his canny encyclopaedic knowledge, and an instinct for screenplay and location.

Lew continued to keep in touch with his Barton friends and family. In 1958/9, his mother had a sweet shop appropriately opposite The Star cinema site, and, in consequence, he was a regular visitor there; his friends recollecting meeting in the large living room at the rear. There is no record of Ted Lewis's writing activities in his time at the Art College from which he graduated in 1960 with a diploma in illustration and graphic design, specialising in advertisement design. His student life was over and he needed to be in the wider world, leaving Barton and Hull behind to work as a graphic journeyman from late 1961. For Lewis, 'the Sixties' had begun, although as his alter ego, Victor Graves, discovered, it was not a world in which jobs in graphic art came easy.

Chapter 11

Jazz Jive

1958 to 1960

Lew had continued to listen to jazz greats and had an extensive collection of Long Playing records (LPs or vinyls). He also read *Melody Maker*, which at that time was giving publicity to staples of UK jazz, including the likes of Ken Colyer, Joe Harriott and Chris Barber, who were the main live players before American musicians arrived on these shores, they being largely discouraged by the US Government from entering the UK until 1962. Ronnie Scott's Club opened in Gerard Street, Soho in 1959. In those days, hitch hiking was a safe, popular method of travel amongst young people, and Lew adopted this means of travel to reach the club, which was becoming a unique venue of the live jazz scene. He little knew then that Soho would be a compulsive haunt of his in later life and yet another seminal influence on his writing.

Jazz, for many years intuitively at Lew's fingers, became increasingly a focal part of his life in his last two years of college. He had played piano in Barton mainly from ear, and following artists he admired and heard on his record collection. He was particularly appreciative of the piano playing of Oscar Peterson, George Shearing and Dave Brubeck, and was lucky to have been able to attend the Dave Brubeck Quartet's first UK concert in 1958 with friends Nick Turner and Lance Waddell. New Orleans jazz was becoming increasingly popular, encouraged by the enthusiasm of Ken Colyer who had been a New Orleans aficionado for many years, frequently visiting that city and famously being deported on one occasion having jumped ship from the ship on which he had been working. Lincolnshire jazz singer Lulu White put Ken up in New Orleans, and still carries on the New Orleans tradition today. Other musicians were forming bands; the most successful being Chris Barber for whom Colyer, at one time, played trumpet. In the late 1950s, young people were becoming increasingly interested, but the trad boom had not yet started. In 1958, a local student, Ron Burnett, whose parents ran The Station Inn on Beverley Road, enrolled as a student at the college and on the same course as Lew, although two years below. Ron was already an experienced trombone player having played with Chas Chesterman's band since the age of fifteen. Jamming in the college hall brought together musicians of a similar interest, so Ron could gather round him a nucleus of college musicians, supplemented with players from other local bands. Lew joined up on piano and Unity Jazz Band was formed.

Unity played traditional or New Orleans jazz, rather than the more modern or cool school that Lew usually favoured. Unity had its first gigs in 1958, with a front line of Tony Dugdale (Doug) on clarinet, Ron Burnett (now still playing, leading the Mardi Gras Band in York and who has enjoyed an auspicious jazz musical life) on trombone and Alan Peacock on trumpet. The rhythm section was usually made up of Paul Shepherdson or Brian Thompson on drums, Eric Dobson or John Harrison on banjo, and, of course, Lew on piano. In an engagingly frank moment, Ron confides that Ted was not a particularly distinguished player at that time, but he was a good draw with 'cool cat' good looks and a perpetual cigarette between his lips. Occasional guest players included the experienced Eric Dobson, Eddie Anderson who later played guitar with Geoff Woodhouse Band, and banjo player Ken Ford, who later, with Sarah, went on to run Hull Jazz Club in modern times before he died in 2017. Lew and Ron became very close friends at college, socially, in japes and in jazz escapades. Ron describes a very real bond between them, which continued for years after their college days and which he still feels to this day.

Unity played regularly at dances in the large hall on the first floor at the college. It also frequently appeared at the original Hull Jazz Club in Windsor Hall in Argyle Street, half a mile down Anlaby Road from the college. Band members were often to be found drinking in the Argyle Hotel before gigs, attracting fans who enjoyed the band members' company. Both the hotel and hall are now demolished. Others' appearances at the club included Mick Mulligan's band, with iconic singer and writer George Melly; Bridlington's Bob Wallace, who later joined up with Hugh Rainey to form the Storyville Jazz Band from 1959; and the Geoff Woodhouse Band. Lance Waddell is one former fan who recounts how friends and followers of the band would descend on his flat in St George's Road off Anlaby Road near to Argyle Street. There they would all change, prepare and meet up with other friends, often at the Argyle Hotel, prior to the gig at the Hull Jazz Club. Soon, there was a regular clique of young men and girls who hung around following Unity, which was encouraged to play as many gigs as possible. Some followers became 'the crowd', others merely hangers on, resulting in strong, lasting bonds of friendship being forged. Lance recalls the occasion he espied a particularly lovely girl across the room, who he immediately believed to be very special and who later became his wife. Nowadays, they both enjoy meeting up with others of the same era to reminisce and celebrate those heady times, particularly at jazz sessions in the Lairgate Hotel at Beverley.

Unity played regularly at weekly sessions in The Olde Blue Bell's upstairs concert room, a venue hiding down a narrow passageway off Lowgate in Hull's Old Town, as well as 'The Scene' in the Astoria Cinema on Holderness Road, where The Temperance Seven also appeared in this heyday of British trad jazz. Lance Waddell describes Lew, floating on its waves of music, often emerging at 6 am from its all-nighters, and, combining work with his cinema habit, having often appeared half asleep at the piano during gigs, iconic cigarette dangling from his lips. No doubt Lew presented as a dangerously endearing, compelling figure to the girls, but the somnolence was not always an act. Unity also played at the Kevin Ballroom above Hull's market on North Church Side, a venue where Roy Tilley's band often appeared.

Regular 'Riverboat Shuffles' on the Humber Ferry, sailing from Hull Corporation Pier were other opportunities for Unity, where the band shared the bill with other bands, including the zany Alberts, which later morphed into the 1920s-style Temperance Seven who peaked with their 1961 hit *"You're Driving Me Crazy"*. Unity trombonist, Ron Burnett, recalls one escapade when the band played a Riverboat Shuffle and Lew had no instrument to play on. There were no electronic pianos, so band members cadged an instrument from a local pub near the pier head, manhandling it the not inconsiderable distance to the *Tattershall Castle* ferry. Describing Riverboat Shuffle events, the real Ron describes the borrowed piano sliding from side to side in the *Tattershall's* saloon – a sight to behold. We can imagine Lew valiantly trying to continue playing with his usual studied insouciance, as always, a fag clamped firmly between his lips. Ted Lewis recalls this, writing *"The pubs around the pier were jam-packed with mobs of people waiting to go on to the Ferry. Already there was a great queue at the barrier, Janet and I walked towards the barrier. Ron [sic] and other members of the band were unloading the drum kit from the trumpet player's car."* There was in fact no member of Unity called Ron in the novel; the fictitious name accorded to Harry, an elementary but unfortunate error, is not unknown in personal-experience fiction. Henry Miller, writing *No Villain* during five days in 1939, described his family's early life in the garment industry including a central character who was clearly himself. From time to time he also forgot the characters' names and substitutes the real ones.

Unity was also a popular band outside Hull, playing at Scarborough (including on boat trips), Bridlington Pavilion, Hessle Town Hall and York, where Ron Burnett now lives with his wife Jenny. Lew's close friend recalls that Unity played Pete Madden's Café in York's High Petergate, and at the final York Arts Ball at the City's Assembly Rooms, which some College students from Hull also attended and would have done so for Unity's next gig but for the Local Authority owner that feared student damage to the Assembly Rooms' distinctive, Oliver-Messel-designed pillars. Incongruous amongst the students at the Assembly Rooms was cigar-smoking Colonel Percy Legard, arrayed in his velvet jacket, and every inch a racehorse owner living in luxurious Leat House, Norton near Malton to which Unity was invited. The band not only played there but enjoyed all the house's facilities, including a summer house and swimming pool, as well as a copiously stocked bar. There, on other visits by the band, they met showbiz personalities who had just been appearing at Yorkshire coastal resorts for most of the summer of 1959, and particularly admired musicians from Cyril Stapleton's Orchestra. Similar colourful escapades feature in both *All the Way Home and All the Night Through* and *The Rabbit*.

Tradition has it that modern bands now travel in beaten up Transit vans. However, these vehicles did not start production until 1965, so, instead, Unity trumpet player Alan Peacock or one of the crowd, Nick Marlin, drove the band to gigs in Alan's father's Humber Super Snipe – an executive saloon so large and comfortable that many were used as military staff cars. If Mr Peacock Senior needed the car for an early 6 am start, the band travelled in one of his horse boxes, often rolling about in the hay. At Nick's suggestion, Unity members later purchased a 1937 Singer Saloon, which was laughingly described as more of a pram. In that vehicle, at twenty-five miles per hour, Unity just made it to Leeds where their one and only recording session took place, laying down five tracks, *"My Daddy Rocks Me"*, *"Travelling Blues"*, *"Marching through Georgia"*, *"Shine"* and *"Black and Blue"*, which have been remastered by Ron Burnett and are available on CD. Lew painted Unity and some of its fans in oil on canvas especially for Nick Marlin whose widow, Jane, still proudly displays it as a treasured possession. The painting shows the band in their characteristic poses, with himself, quietly to one side, facing away from the viewer. Lewis is not known to have been a band member after his Hull days nor did he play professionally; his talent put on ice, destined never to have been developed further save for treasured private performances. He did, however, delight in playing piano in pubs and friends' homes when the mood took him.

By this time in his life, Lew's natural liquid intake and character was now consolidating, with friends realising that he was a permanent compelling influence on those around him. He was, however, chronically unsure of his appearance and, indeed, Judy Burnett, unlike others who were smitten, says she found him unprepossessing. Lew underlines his insecurity in the words of Victor Graves in *The Rabbit: "Too many hours spent in practising smiling from all angles in front of my dressing-table mirror has convinced me of the futility of trying to enhance my charm by opening my mouth; already over proportioned jowls circulating with the action of chewing could hardly accentuate my appeal!"* Throughout all his life Lew would often also present as unassuming, quiet, but also full of natural charm. Despite his insecurity, he was usually personable unless drunk, in which case he could become unpleasant. Friends, neighbours, acquaintances and business contacts alike have commented *"he was a lovely man"*, *"he was always lovely"*, *"he was good to be with"*, *"he was wonderful company"* and *"he had a special, quiet wit"*.

Chapter 12

A Graphic Description

Career in Graphics 1961 to 1965

Real life and fiction merged after Ted Lewis (now often called Ted, especially after he used that appellation in his novels) qualified in graphic art. He expected to find his natural talents, sharpened by his lectures, practise and study, to be easily in demand, but this was not to be. Not every enterprise wished to employ a young graduate with precious little experience in business, a lesson hard learned by both Victor Graves and Ted. Both had returned home in 1960 to seek work, but there was no immediate reward for graduating. Ted, who attained the age of twenty-one on 15th January 1961, celebrated whilst in Barton with family and such friends as remained in the area. He ultimately found employment, of course; first in commercial graphics at the newly Government-supported Westland Helicopters in Yeovil, Somerset. This company had been forged from Bristol, Fairey and Saunders-Roe, and had become highly successful until the UK Government decided to purchase helicopters from America causing Defence Secretary Michael Heseltine to give one of his dramatic resignations. Despite enquiry, even with the daughter of the then managing director, unfortunately, no examples of Ted Lewis's graphic work there have been located.

Although there is no record of this first known commercial work, Ted found freelance projects in the literary scene as an artist providing illustrations for children's books; the first example of which is in Alan Delgado's 1962 children's book *The Hot Water Bottle Mystery.* Although he did not draw the dust-cover illustration, a task often self-allocated to publishers, Ted did provide them within the novel itself, with graphics credited to 'Edward Lewis' inside the novel, which is still available from second-hand booksellers. Initial payment for these book illustrations was £70, which, legend has it, enabled Ted to travel to London so he could advance his career. Ted also left Westland under something of a cloud, not entirely unrelated to alcohol. Happily he secured another appointment on the in-house company magazine of Dexion Ltd, whose premises were in the Enfield borough that geographically straddles the northeast of London. The company was a household name, and a then privately owned company manufacturing eponymous steel shelving; in 1962 it had a substantial turnover of £5.7M – another highly successful employer. This position enabled Ted Lewis to move in with his childhood friend John Dickinson in his Chalk Farm flat, 19 miles away from Enfield. However, the degree of their youthful relationship is shown in Ted's first novel: *"Phillip* [John] *and I had always been close."* They were *so* close that Ted recorded that their conversation was trusting and confidential, as exemplified by a pithy comment from *"Phillip"*: *"It seems to me that the only problem is yourself."* Whilst his friend, Lew also had an interest in science at school; John had developed his early grammar school special interest in biology, and soon determined on a career as a doctor, later continuing his studies at Guy's Hospital in 'The Smoke' (the slang expression for London insisted upon as a chapter heading by Ted in his last novel *GBH*).

Ted Lewis began to be in demand, providing graphics to the advertising industry, and subsequently joining Butterfield's Advertising Agency, but while doing so he continued to supplement his income with other freelance graphic work. He was also writing his first novel, although he proved to be an undisciplined worker, having a variety of distractions as a serial drinker with a fascination with fleshpots of Soho as well as closer, personal, fleshly experiences with several casual girlfriends. The Chalk Farm flat, which was also shared with Ted's childhood friend Mike Shucksmith and Unity clarinet player Tony Dugdale, was six stations away from the Tottenham Court Road London Underground station, which was adjacent to Soho. That magnetic area, seething with a rich variety of human enjoyment and every kind of leisure experience, was effectively nearly outside Ted's back door. He worked very late, often all through the night, to keep up with commitments and aspirations. He sold graphics for *Alice in Wonderland*, amongst a variety of other book illustrations, as well as illustrating BBC graphic panels for children's TV shows. Edging towards films, his work also included graphics for *Bridge over the River Kwai*, although, to date, there has been no success in recovering these for publication.

Ted's friend and flatmate completed his hospital training and qualified as Dr John Dickinson, with aspirations to become a GP. He had met his future wife, Nadine, in Pimlico and married her in 1963. Lewis, with no steady girlfriend at the time, attended the wedding; characteristically painting a portrait of Nadine as their wedding present. John's bride's Belgian parents had initially moved to England on business, but then returned to Ghent only to come back to live in England permanently. The oil painting shows Nadine, who worked in dress design, and had once worked briefly for actress and film star Joan Collins, pictured in relief against a background of the Humber Estuary, showing the haunts where John and Ted used to play as lads. *"This will be your new home,"* the painting seems to say, *"the place that I myself most love."* With that painting serving almost as a prophesy, the Dickinsons, who were then unaware of Ted's serious writing ambitions, soon decided on making a return to Barton upon Humber, where John was offered a position as a GP in the amalgamated group practice at Central Surgery in Barton, later becoming a partner for the rest of his professional life. Group practices were a comparatively new concept, very much advocated by Dr Tom Kirk of Barton, whose wartime diaries and advocacy of the National Health Service picked him out as a local medical giant. The practice also included Dr John Ball who was later to become Ted's doctor when the novelist returned to Barton. After 1974, John also befriended the novelist when Ted Lewis was especially depressed. Dr John Dickinson spent the rest of his professional life in the town; he was approachable and sought after by his patients. He was nicknamed 'The Running Man' by friends, as he had a predilection for what we now call jogging; an active man in stark contrast to Ted's lack of interest in outdoor sport.

For a second time, therefore, John moved away from where his friend was living; although in the final years of Ted Lewis' life, they resumed contact, with the writer appreciating that fellowship following his final return to his roots in 1974. In the interim, although living in London, Lewis continued to visit Barton, where not only did he have childhood friends, but his parents as well. In 1964, Ted's friend, Neil Ashley, purchased Highfield House, an imposing, partially timbered house standing in an imposing position at the end of Westfield Road, giving it astonishing views over the Humber Estuary. Nowadays, visitors and walkers following the *Ted Lewis Trail* can stand at this vantage point and take in the still-spectacular views across the graceful Humber Bridge, the bank's conservation and nature areas, and the town's new developments. Furthermore, present-day walkers going west along

Westfield Road need to walk through a dingy underpass; the A15 Humber Bridge Approach Road having cut Westfield Road in half. A thunder of trunk traffic replaces the peace of Lewis's early years, but the view remains encapsulated in one of Lewis's best oil paintings. In Neil's front room, the artist's brushes created an expansive view of the countryside and river, free of later development; the place of adventures, and a backdrop to the finale of one of Ted Lewis's most famous stories, *Get Carter*. These were places that had given him freedom and adventure in earlier days, and in painting the scene he did so in a way reminiscent of Cezanne, who often focussed on the area he loved, the mountain of Montagne Sainte-Victoire, to which he tramped and painted faithfully for three years.

Had Ted Lewis concentrated on cartoon and graphic work, he would certainly have had the skills to produce iconic cartoons as did his contemporary (born the same year as Ted), the legendary graphic artist Ken Harrison. That famous Barton cartoonist was responsible for drawing *Minnie the Minx* and *Desperate Dan* amongst many others as part of the D C Thompson stable. Ted arguably also had the talent to enjoy the success his arts college contemporary, David Remfry, did. However, he elected another path.

Chapter 13

First Novel as Ted Lewis

1958 to 1965

Ted Lewis used his experiences at Hull School of Art and Design, particularly from 1958 when he was eighteen, as the entire basis of his first novel *All the Way Home and All the Night Through*, which was published in 1965, but upon which Ted Lewis had been working during the previous years when making a hesitating living from graphic art. The novel has a clumsy title, like the 1959 Alan Sillitoe novel *The Loneliness of the Long Distance Runner*, but Ted's title described the burning-a-candle-at-both-ends lifestyle he lived. The background Ted drew upon was his days with Unity Jazz Band, his casual encounters with a significant number of women in his life, the fellowship of true friends and an emotional affair with a very special girl. That girl fascinated him largely because she was seemingly unapproachable, remote from his own social strata and the mores of other students who surrounded him.

Ted Lewis began the novel by writing sensitively about his love for his home town, Barton, his relish for Hull and its student environs, as well as opportunities for drinking to excess and student escapades. He espies Janet Walker, in real life the daughter of a well-to-do couple in Kirkella, an expensive suburb of Hull, in whom he feigns only slight interest. Harry casually points out *"a couple of dollies worth keeping in sight."* Victor nevertheless goes on to discuss the girl in detail, *"You notice a lot seeing as how you don't find her attractive."* Harry is in no doubt about his initial impression of Janet's companion: *"Jenny I think. Dead cute, she is, you know, all coy smiles."* Janet's character was modelled on Juliet Hiden, recounts Judy Burnett, who should know for Jenny in the book was modelled on Judy who in turn is now married to Ron Burnett (Harry). Janet, does not present as a typical student. She dresses and behaves in a reserved and rather demure way, which fascinated Victor/Ted. For Victor, seduction of such a girl was a specific challenge; for Janet, there was an edge, and her own challenge or escape in a romance with such an acknowledged lothario. Their needs and experiences are transmuted to almost obsessive love, fanned by explorative sexual experience. Heather

Bowen, now Heather Wilson living in Australia, was also one of Lew's demure conquests in his college days, so he plainly needed that kind of challenge. Of one dust cover of *All the Way Home and All the Night Through* showing a salacious picture of a lustful scene, Heather is keen to distance her character and, indeed, another dust cover does show a more retiring and conventional young girl. The novel has been described as, at best, a gauche and naïve account of an immature student's life, and Ron Burnett feels that it was not well written. Certainly, Ted was disappointed that his first novel was not the huge commercial success he expected. Ron and Judy Burnett say that the events unfold in the novel as accurately as a diary of their student lives at that time.

The Janet/Victor relationship founders in predictable disaster when drunken jealousy leads to Victor assaulting Janet and the inevitable breakdown of the relationship, which he later also returned to in his 1975 novel *The Rabbit*. The particularly poignant and instructive event occurs when Victor lashes out at Janet blindly. After goading the girl about his misplaced fears of infidelity Victor records *"She tried to push me away ... I gripped her more tightly ... she sobbed ... the final red of my trembling violence burned into my eyes and I hit her across the mouth and pushed her as hard as I could into the bedroom wall ... Everything snapped back in my mind ... My mouth hung open at the comprehension of the last few minutes ... I gripped her with all my strength and pulled her over to the bed, pushing her down on it. 'I didn't mean to hurt you Janet you know I love you.'"* Here is an insightful, accurate, no-holds-barred or excused account of the demon testosterone, which is perched on an otherwise controlled male. So understanding is he of the condition, that Ted Lewis could recount male brutality and abuse as just an aside to gritty life, just as if he was the master puppeteer and violence was his stringed Pinocchio.

In Britain, today, women are largely recognised as having mostly climbed out of accepting the treadmill of previously accepted violence. Part of the recent history of Hull, where Ted's novel is set, involves a major women's struggle to be free and their consequences. During 1968, in Ted Lewis's old Hull haunts, trawlermen's wives had emerged from their subservient moulds by securing safety at sea without the help and often the knowledge of their menfolk, who later turned on them for caring. The *Headscarf Revolutionaries*, a book in which author Dr B Lavery recounts the determination of Lillian Bilocca and other Hull trawlermen's wives, and shows that if women can cope with abuse and break out of their cages, nothing will induce them to return. Sadly, in most of his noir crime novels, Lewis preferred to show those victims continually denied that freedom, after being punched senseless. Aside from the emotion, the novel describes much of Lewis's exploits as a jazzer, and his relationship with girls who alternatively use or adore him. Gauche as Victor Graves may be, it is also a description of the uncertainties existent in the lives of those who may well seem otherwise well assured, and Jo Lewis, Ted Lewis's wife, later put it on record that it was her husband's uncertainties that coloured much of his life.

The novelist recorded in his diary, which was recovered from a charity stall after Bertha's death by Barton's Jack Thorpe, that Ted finished this novel on his birthday, 15th January 1964. Optimistically, he recorded his intention to start another novel on 2nd March of that year. That second book was not, as one might suppose, *Jack's Return Home*, which was his second published novel. Although the diary does not record it, it is likely that the second project was one entitled *Two-Sided Triangle*, an account of a newly married couple. Commentators have suggested that this was an account of Ted's own marriage, but he did not meet his future wife until 1966. *All the Way Home and All the Night Through* was serialised in *Petticoat* girls' magazine, but Ted Lewis needed to find a publisher for the whole novel. He had the advantage of still being in touch with his mentor, Henry Treece, whose assistance he sought. Treece was able introduce the manuscript to his own literary agent at that time, John Johnson, who succeeded in interesting Hutchinson's publishing house in the novel as part of an initiative in 1957. New Authors Limited started by publishing first books from Commonwealth writers, but later enlarged its scope. An author received a £150 advance and a percentage of royalties. The company was non-profit making, although Hutchinson received a substantial 25% management fee. Ted's novel was accepted and published.

Of some amusement was a note about the author in the first edition saying, *"He writes between 10 pm and 2 am three nights a week"*, whereas we have seen his work pattern was more haphazard. Although *The Times'* reviewer referred to the work as a *"fresh and original book"*, it had faint praise amongst critics, such as *"The rough pattern of his personality that pokes through his writing and his talk are attractive" (Books and Bookman)*, so the novel achieved disappointing sales. Initially the hardback (it never appeared as a paperback) featured that illustration of a supposed demure Janet, but only later, perhaps to stimulate sales, a more alluring cover featured a wide-throated young lady in the throes of a supposed ecstatic embrace. Some first editions are still at large, and with a dust jacket they retail at around £700 at today's prices.

All the Way Home and All the Night Through, although fairly criticised as gauche or self-indulgent, as well as demonstrating Lewis's inherent self-doubt, which he later poured into the character of Jack Carter, also gives an early prediction the writer's own slavery to drink – his ultimate downfall: *"I felt sober but I knew I shouldn't because I knew I shouldn't because I had been drinking fairly regularly for the past two hours ... Thoughts of futility and irrational suspicion were weaving dully into my mind."*

Chapter 14

Film Graphics

1965 to 1968

Writing was clearly not then a reliable source of income, and whilst Ted Lewis did expect instant success, it did not come, and friends say he continued to be disappointed and perplexed. Fortunately, his career as a textual graphic artist was not only peaking, but destined to change direction. It was also becoming difficult to combine that work with his ultimate creativity as a writer, as well as enjoying life, particularly in Soho.

In 1965 Ted resigned from his job with Butterfield's Advertising Agency; the year *All the Way Home and All the Night Through* was published. Using his now proven experience, he turned to his beloved film industry for work, achieving a position with Halas and Butler in 1966. This was also the year in which he married. Ted had just met and fallen in love with the attractive Josephine Roome (Jo), an advertising personal assistant (PA) who also worked and lived at the Moscow Arms near to where Ted's future literary agent, (The Hon) Toby Eady, had his rooms. The pub was, coincidentally, a one-time drinking hole of actor/comedians, Peter Sellers and Spike Milligan, and, again, as a plaque on the building shows, Milligan worked in the same building where Toby Eady subsequently began his agency business. Lewis married Jo on 17th September 1966, after a short courtship, at the Parish Church in Bayswater. All the main guests, including special friends Ron Burnett, Dr John Dickinson, Unity 'stick' (liquorice stick/clarinet) player Tony Dugdale, and Tony Peacock, were in formal top hat and tails, although band members had once worn a trademark waistcoat uniform. A serial lothario, Lewis evidently now felt more settled, and film work was now nearer his grasp. The couple started married life in a flat, fittingly above a cinema, in Belsize Park. One important wedding guest was sadly absent, however, for on 10th June 1966 young Lew's mentor, Henry Treece, had died. Only in the May of that year had he come to Lambeth, not far from where Ted lived, to deliver a lecture at the new children's library on South Island. It was one of Treece's last speaking engagements and, undoubtedly, he would have been a central guest at the wedding had he survived. However, Ted had tangibly rewarded the early promise that Treece recognised in his young, rebellious pupil. There was no more mentoring from a literary or personal standpoint from that source; Lewis was then on his own, although in many respects his new literary agent would take over Treece's mantle. Jo was aware that Ted was a drinker, but for many years did not appreciate that he had a very real addiction problem, and had already been drinking frequently and to excess in Soho.

Ted's new employer, Halas and Batchelor, based, coincidentally, in Lewes, was the country's largest and most influential producer of animated films, with a reputation of pioneering new styles and techniques, as well as discovering or nurturing new talent. Halas had been contracted to Format Films of Hollywood, which produced the animated version of that classic TV western *The Lone Ranger*, of which there were ninety instalments in all. Lewis was engaged as a background artist for this series, which ran on CHS; the last episode being shown on 9th March 1968, by which time Ted has moved on. He was also writing the novel that was to make his name. Jez Stewart, animation curator of The British Film Institute, cannot identify Ted Lewis's work precisely but opines of *The Lone Ranger, "It was a most extraordinarily well designed series."* Its subject must have given Lewis much pleasure, given his passion for animation and other westerns. From the description given by Stewart, Lewis was plainly part of a team that excelled. One of the design team in the series with Lewis was one Tom Barling.

In 1967, Lewis, ironically with a perpetual fag in his mouth, was responsible at Halas for graphics in the public health cartoon film *Dying for a Smoke*, the object of which was to warn the public of the dire dangers of such smoking! At the time of writing, *Dying for a Smoke* is still available online. 'Starring' fictional old Nick O'Teen (voice over by an uncredited Warren Mitchell TV star of *'Til Death us do Part*) and Sam Sucker, it followed up the 1965 ban on TV cigarette advertising. Plainly, it had no influence on the creator's smoking habit, which had started in childhood, was endemic in his home and haunts, and continued unabated throughout his life. Ted Lewis is nevertheless a name shown proudly in the credits. Now a film graphic journeyman, Ted's recognised skills enabled him to move forward in the industry to his last and most prestigious position, reputedly with the encouragement and recommendation of Tom Barling of Halas. Lewis was appointed by TVC (Television Cartoons Ltd) as animation clean-up supervisor on The Beatles' ground-breaking, surreal, animated musical comedy, *Yellow Submarine*, a production that was very much the brainchild of multitalented, respected graphic designer Heinz Edelman.

There were some sixty-four animators working on a *Yellow Submarine*, drawing original characters or other created images. Each animation artist, naturally, has his or her own personal style. A clean-up animator draws together these versions or 'roughs' and produces a drawing maquette or template that all images must relate to, and therefore has a highly responsible, pivotal and crucial role in any production. Lewis, who shouldered these substantial responsibilities dwelling in *Submarine's* fictitious Pepperland, dealing with the dreaded Blue Meanies, and rubbing graphic shoulders with characters of the likes of Phud and Nowhere Man. Released in July 1968, *Yellow Submarine* was a box office hit, and is still recognised as an icon of its genre; the images of which are still popular. There is, of course, an eponymous replica of the graphically drawn submarine at John Lennon Airport in Speke on the outskirts of Liverpool; a very real, appropriate image of Lewis's graphic work that would endure. There can be no doubt that working in the creative atmosphere of *Yellow Submarine* creation would have delighted Ted's penchant for irreverent cartoon graphics, as well as being embedded in film work, and, of course, he was also being well remunerated. He was, like the *Yellow Submarine*, on the top of his graphic *Aztec Hill*. Whilst Ted continued to sketch for his own pleasure and the pleasure of others, he did not return to commercial graphic art, for his literary artistry was ready to take over and his fascination with films would be fulfilled by watching his words brought to their different life on films sets dedicated to his work.

Chapter 15

Soho

Living a Life on the Edge, 1961 to 1974

Soho remained Ted's abiding haunt, variously from 1962 to 1974, providing him also with material and characterisations for a rich collection of successful crime novels. Then, as now, Soho consists of the traditionally named square mile bounded by Oxford Street, Leicester Square, Charing Cross Road and Regent Street to the west, and includes the area known as 'Chinatown', which sits between Leicester Square and Shaftesbury Avenue. It buzzed with artistic and pleasurable activity, and experiences beloved of writers, musicians and entrepreneurs. In that atmosphere, revelled painters Lucian Freud, Francis Bacon, dissolute writer Jeffrey Barnard (famously 'indisposed'), photographers John Deakin and Harrison Marks, and poet Dylan Thomas. The drinking culture was endemic amongst artists, in which milieu Ted Lewis thrived. He could slip into this society comparatively inconspicuously, participating through the drinks in his glass with which he was well familiar, enjoying an osmosis of colourful activity that was to emerge in print with complete credibility. There were historic and other pubs aplenty that he drank in, several with artistic and literary histories, such as The George, Pillars of Hercules, Three Greyhounds and French House (the haunt of Dylan Thomas). Then there was The Dog and Duck, a pub that could almost have been deliberately selected by Lewis as a heritage, for George Orwell, John Constable and Dante Gabriel Rossetti were habitués. Although, in the 1960s, Ted Lewis was, only a literary one-trick pony. When friend and fellow jazzer Ron Burnett came to London for work purposes, they would enjoy these haunts; Ron pleased to stay in the communal flat and once managing entry to the Colony Club to rub shoulders with some of the drinking artistic elite.

The Street Offences Act 1959 had driven many working girls off the streets and alleys, hence there grew up a plethora of red-lit doorbells, announcements of 'French Lessons', 'Model Agency' or 'Therapist', and it was also estimated that there were in the region of nearly a hundred 'walk ups' or strip clubs. The Metropolitan Police ('The

Met') boasted a Vice Squad and a Flying Squad, but whilst organised crime sold protection elsewhere, in Soho a sex industry business was often protected by a network of corrupt police officers. In that way, some drinking clubs were fronts for prostitution, for if you had The Met in your pocket, shady entrepreneurs could get away with bending or completely flaunting the law to hoover up large profits.

At the same time as tarts moved off the streets, Soho became acceptable for ordinary women and girls to visit due to the emergence of coffee bars from the late 1950s, and an explosion of interest in young people's music as well as jazz. It was in the year of 'The Act' that saxophone player and impresario Ronnie Scott had opened his basement virtual jazz speakeasy in Gerrard Street, which Ted Lewis had visited as a student before it moved to its ultimate home in Frith Street in 1965. Clubs such as Marquee, Flamingo and La Discotheque featured rhythm and blues, popular and disco dance music, and became the resort of many young people enjoying what became known as the 'Swinging Sixties'. Club 100 in Wardour Street show-pieced an enthusiasm for jazz. Sexual liberation was also a hallmark of this period, despite sexual intercourse beginning, occurring, according to Philip Larkin *"between the 'Chatterly ban' and the Beatles' first LP."* That remark which has is the iconic phrase from the sixties came from *Annus Mirabalis in High Windows*, although, like Larkin whose sexual experience reputedly actually began in 1948, Lewis's journey into the joys of sex also started earlier than his first fiction.

Back in 1960, club owners Michael Klinger and Tony Tenser had set up London's first members-only sex cinema, the Compton Cinema Club; an event and an interest that was to have huge significance for Ted Lewis. In Gerrard Street, George Harrison Marks had already set up his studio as photographer of nudes and a publisher of what we now call soft porn magazines, subsequently producing a succession of explicit comedies. As early as 1957 he published *Kamera*, and Klinger co-produced one of Marks' first legal girlie films, *Naked as Nature Intended*. Marks was not only well known to Lewis in the environs of Soho, but amongst other literati. In 1961, the George Harrison Marks film *The Window Dresser*, starring Pamela Green completely unclothed, had been the subject of an obscene publications prosecution, which the judge threw out. Lewis showed his spare, effective style as well as an understanding of the portrayal of revealing couture when he wrote in *Jack's Return Home "The girl called Joy brought me my drink. She was strictly Harrison Marks".* Writing from Hull to the magazine Conquest, Philip Larkin later wrote *"So you're a Harrison Marks Man"* during a correspondence column exchange on the effects of eroticism.

In 1966, the British Board of Film Censors, as it then was, passed, uncut, some explicit scenes in *Alfie*, which coincidentally starred Michael Caine who was also the star of Lewis's *Get Carter*. At the time Ted was around, more hard-core pornographic films (sometimes referred to as 'rollers') were illegally swilling around Soho with significant profits filling criminals' pockets – often funding otherwise legitimate businesses that were sometimes fronted by high-profile entrepreneurs or trusted celebrities. A good number of film images were only a little less explicit than those currently available more freely on the Internet. Even then, however, producers were seeking ways in which more racy material could be introduced into mainstream British films to push out their boundaries. Klinger was one who had an interest in the profits to be made this way.

On 6th November 1960, Penguin Books was tried for alleged obscenity in D H Lawrence's novel, *Lady Chatterley's Lover*. The jury found for the defendant in a result that ushered in the liberalization of publishing, and which some saw as the beginning of the permissive society in Britain. The early 1960s then produced more explicit 'kitchen sink' dramas. Alan Sillitoe's 1960 *Saturday Night and Sunday Morning* told of a young factory worker in Nottingham having an affair with a married woman; the penalty for making her pregnant being a beating from her husband. *A Taste of Honey* in 1962 was about a seventeen-year-old daughter of a crude, sexually indiscriminate, alcoholic mother. This teenager also gets pregnant and is abandoned. In Stan Barstow's *A Kind of Loving*, a Manchester factory draughtsman has sex with Ingrid, a typist who also works for the same employer. He proposes marriage when the girl becomes pregnant, and the couple move in with the girl's domineering mother, who disapproves of the match. The typist has a miscarriage, her lover regrets, comes home drunk and the couple then consider the possibility of making do with 'a kind of loving'.

Ted could visit Soho and its environs as a carefree, single, young man from 1962, when he was twenty-two, until the year of his marriage in 1966, when he was twenty-six. While he was focussed on obtaining a publisher for his first local novel, set in Lincolnshire and Yorkshire, he was still absorbing the Soho atmosphere for it was to be an essential, useful background for his crime novels. Ted's later written account that *"Jack's Return Home was set in a world I knew nothing about"* was singularly disingenuous. The scene was set, not only for Lewis to begin, finish and find a publisher for his revival of the dark crime novel he was writing in the later 1960s, and which had a plot with explicit sexual overtones. Dark or noir novels by British writers had become popular in the 1930s, but this genre ceded to American noir pulp fiction after World War II. Not only did Lewis write his second published novel *Jack's Return Home* reviving the British tradition that had largely grown out of popularity but he found it converted into celluloid starring no less than film's rising hot property, Michael Caine.

As Henry James wrote of Soho "*All human life is here.* "; a quotation that subsequently appeared on the News of the World masthead without attribution. The full quotation was in fact from Henry James' *The Madonna of the Future, "Cats and monkeys, monkeys and cats, all human life is here"* Unlike the proverbial *News of the World* reporter (since press intrusion, a comedy figure of the past), Lewis never made excuses and rarely left. Early in his marriage, and with a child on the way and born in 1968, the scenario needed to be readjusted. From writing *Jack's Return Home* in 1970 to his last novel, *GBH*, in 1980, Lewis used the pornography industry as a background to most of his crime novels; the profit from which was often one of the principal motivations of many of the gangster characters he created. In the 1960s, Soho was buzzing and Ronnie Scott's was jumping – perfect haunts for a man with eclectic jazz tastes, a wide appetite for alcohol-fuelled enjoyment and the practical experience of playing in a band.

In 1963 that British jazz scene had been celebrated by the release of the film *All Night Long*, an Othello-style plot with its background of jealousy. This was an immediate turn on for Lewis and there are clear references to its style in the Lewis's books taken the film sets that were a background to the action. The principal character in *All Night Long* was jazz drummer Johnny Cousin, played by the brooding, often-sardonic Patrick McGoohan who, five years later, found greater fame in TVs *The Prisoner*. McGoohan learned to play the drums for his part in the film, just as the young Ted Lewis had learned how to use the sticks to extend his piano playing skills in his Unity Jazz Band days. *All Night Long* also features many players with whom Ted would have been familiar at Scott's, including bass player Kenny Napper, trumpet and ensemble leader Stan Roderick, drummer Alan Ganley and pianist Colin Purbrook. The film also celebrated American icons Charlie Mingus and, Ted's favourite, Dave Brubeck. Pert, blond, leggy singer Marty Stevens in *All Night Long* was the necessary 'sex interest'; a prequel to the bed-writhing cameo appearance of Britt Ekland (*"I only took the part and my clothes off because I was broke"*) as Anna in *Get Carter*, which was one of her seventy-three film credits. The style of locations in *All Night Long* included opulently converted, trendy, split-level, spacious living with music areas in an old industrial building having gadgets slipping silently from walls on command. In many a Ted Lewis novel there is a graphic reprise of *All-Night-Long*-style locations and reference to the then jazz scene. For example, in *GBH* Ted writes *"When you walk into the lounge this window is to the right ... climb the open-tread staircase to the room's second, broader level ... at the room's far end you would be faced by brickwork ... a small open fireplace aluminium trimmed ... two movie projectors ... the drinks supply, the stereo ... jet black grand piano ... a panel of switches, one of which operates the movie screen ... March wind blusters." And in Jack Carter and the Mafia Pigeon "The room I am in is all Swedish ... the slightly sunken bit in the middle line with low white leather settees with the backs reaching the normal floor level ... honey coloured floor ... scattered furs ... plain white desk that is worth half an Aston Martin."*

Although married, Ted was still enjoying his haunts in Soho. It was not necessary to be Hercule Poirot to detect how Soho worked either; *"If you need a fast, executive car, go to West End Central CID"* was a joke by-line by police officers needing to circumvent official transport, turning a blind eye to the corruption that was largely unrecognised in mainstream society, despite being a necessary hand-in-glove for underworld activities. Criminals, tarts, hangers-on and police, all *dramatis personae* of the underworld, rubbed shoulders with Ted Lewis and popped up in his crime. The alert observer, Ted Lewis, stripped them bare, exploiting them in language. Talk abounded following the dramatic trials, awash as it then was with talk of controlling criminal gangs, particularly the East End Krays and South/West London Richardsons. Although they had little influence in Soho, which largely survived on police corruption, they formed a useful template for Lewis's first crime novel, with amused contempt of such gangsters understanding a tight and confident criminal society. It was all a fascinating experience and a gift to a creative writer.

Chapter 16

At last, Real Success

Jack's Return Home, 1968 to 1971

Ted Lewis's best-known, seminal novel was not published until 1970, five years after his first and four years after he married. It has been suggested that, after his major earner, *Yellow Submarine*, in 1968, he needed a second income stream, hence another, but more compelling, novel. There was, of course, a financial as well as a literary impetus to write. A successful pot boiler might provide the necessary funds for his new family as the couple were trying for a child, and, thus, their first daughter, Nancy, was born. Ted wrote, sometimes over a thousand words a day, into exercise books, with the text later being typed by Jo. Although, later he did use a typewriter. After the initial chapters had been accepted for publication and film rights, Ted said there was a rush to finish the rest, and he had it completed in three weeks with Jo's assistance and encouragement.

The electric Soho atmosphere was a subconscious inspiration for Ted Lewis to personify a gangland enforcer. He described how he came to write his second novel in a handwritten draft for a later magazine article: *"Only the settings were known to me, settings which I'd responded to when I was being subjected to the influence* [of Raymond Chandler and American films]. *I had to pretend to be the central character, imitate his mannerisms, think ... The ideal of the book came from absolutely nowhere. I was scribbling on a train looking out at the idyllic rural landscape and I thought, for no good reason whatsoever 'Suppose I wrote a book about this criminal whose brother gets murdered and the criminal sets about finding the murderer. I went back home and wrote ... Weekend in Scunthorpe ... Funeral in Scunthorpe ... Gangster's Return."*

Public interest in salacious activity had also been stoked in the early 1960s by the antics of Stephen Ward, John Profumo, Christine Keeler and Mandy Rice-Davies; the latter being a former dancer in night clubs with which Lewis would have been familiar, and which gangsters owned or controlled. He again wrote what he then knew about –the real sex and violence around him. Actor Ray Winstone, also an East End boy, only just born in the year *Yellow Submarine* appeared, tells of his father who boxed with the Kray twins, enabling him to *"play the East End as it really was"*. Likewise, Ted, also a non-participant in crime, accurately described thugs and gangsters. Lewis sent summaries of the plot to his literary agent, John Johnson, who was not impressed. Later he was to suggest the work was not only too explicit but illiterate. Plainly, Lewis was perfectly literate, but his language was clipped and not always in the received-English mode usually experienced by a nation used to a diet of BBC Received Pronunciation (RP). Even dialect was only emerging stealthily from the time of 1960's *Saturday Night and Sunday Morning*. Johnson neither could nor would place the novel.

Ted Lewis later wrote *"This left me depressed, particularly as I still hadn't resolved the majority of the book. By accident I met another agent* [Toby Eady, later of Toby Eady Associates of Orme Court in Bayswater] *who asked to see what I'd written so I sent him what I had. He phoned immediately after reading it full of enthusiasm and asking to read the rest. I promised him the finished book inside three weeks. I must have been mad. My wife and I sat down and worked out the remainder of the book and somehow, I managed to finish inside the three weeks. Finally, a week later, the book had been accepted by a publisher."*

Ted Lewis had an affinity with Eady, the youngest son of writer Mary Wesley, later married to Chinese author Xinran, and a man who had his foot on the first steps of literary agency. They remained thus as novelist and agent all Lewis's life. Toby Eady maintains that no biographer will ever know Ted as well as he did. He found *Jack's Return Home* in its completed form innovative, gripping and of ground-breaking literary quality, so he set about finding a publisher. He contacted Peter Day of Michael Joseph Ltd who also recognised *Jack's Return Home* as special. To avoid blue pencil and encourage acceptance, Day read aloud passages from the novel to his boss in a manner that proved to be acceptable, and thus avoiding him reading the parts that might not have been so acceptable. However, in the first instance, *Jack's Return Home* was sold as a film right in 1969 to Soho nightclub owner Michael Klinger for £10,000, with a real value today of over £140,000 but having an economic power of double that. The average house price was then £5,000. Toby Eady had completed a sweet deal for Ted Lewis, providing the young novelist with real satisfaction, not only because it afforded him recognition but particularly as he had been steeped in films from such an early age and wrote visualising the action almost as a film script. Eady also had numerous acquaintances from Soho, including James Morton, solicitor/crime writer, and others who would sometimes turn up with minders. Toby Eady did, however, have a keen, literary, scholarly ability and a capacity to select writing of quality.

Two books, William Hall's biography of Michael Caine and Andrew Spicer's of Michael Klinger give some insight into how the film emerged. Tony Eady and Hodges in his interviews have confirmed much of what is known. Ted Lewis and Toby Eady enjoyed each other's company and the often-sleazy atmosphere of Soho, and consequently met Klinger in the Dean Street/Compton Street Soho area. Klinger wanted to hold more sway as a film producer. He was a purveyor of girlie films and no stranger to rollers, but had also produced Roman Polanski's first English speaking films, *Cul-de-Sac* and *Repulsion*. Furthermore, he was particularly alert to the public's interest in the recent Kray/Richardson trials and the portrayal of ruthless gangsters. The image of Ronnie Kray brazenly marching into the Blind Beggar and blasting the boastful George Cornell at the bar with a handgun stuck in the imagination of many an otherwise peaceful newspaper reader. In reality, characters such as George Cornell, Jack the Hat and Mad Frankie Frazer were not uncommon in London, but not so much in Soho as it was The Met's patch.

When Klinger purchased the film rights to *Jack's Return Home*, he was already aware of the television work of Mike Hodges, who had produced and directed two feature-length TV thrillers, *Suspect* and *Rumour*. He wrote to Hodges on 27th January 1970, enclosing the script. Hodges was impressed and agreed to direct, although he is said to have received only a £7,000 fee. They could not have envisaged that they were on the way to making what has been recognised as one of the best noir gangster films ever made. It was first proposed that Ian Hendry should play the part of ruthless enforcer Jack Carter, but Klinger preferred Michael Caine, who had already earned credit with a bad-boy image when he played Alfie, which was the second-most popular film at the British box office in 1966 and won a Golden Globe award. Caine, whose career success had been hard fought, felt he could to play Jack Carter accurately by drawing on his own background in the East End, which brought him onto contact with many rough characters. Caine's own chauvinist father, a hugely tough, strong Billingsgate porter with a prodigious capacity for drink, despite being no gangster, was a clear template for how to play Carter. Klinger and Hodges decided to rename the film as *Get Carter*. Filming started apace and was completed at the end of July 1970, after only forty-five shooting days. The events were momentous for Ted Lewis, but also hugely significant for UK crime fiction, which had not seen as gritty a novel as *Jack's Return Home* in recent times. It was first published in hardback by Joseph in 1970, then by Pan Books in 1971 as *Carter* following the film's public acclamation and box office success. It was subsequently reprinted in paperback by Allison & Busby as *Get Carter* with the iconic film shot of Michael Caine wielding the shotgun, just as Ted Lewis had all those years before at The Old Cements in Barton. In the event, Michael Klinger, Michael Caine and Mike Hodges came together to form the 3M company (three Mikes) to exploit their respective talents. Building on the kiln bricks of *Get Carter*, their next venture was *Pulp*, directed by Roman Polanski, but it was not a success. Caine hated filming it, although it brought him into contact with Shakira, to whom he was married in 1973, remaining as constant as Ted Lewis found it impossible to do in his own life.

Ted Lewis's second novel features ruthless enforcer, Jack Carter, who returns to his birthplace of Doncaster, although Lewis based most of the scenarios on the area he knew best, which was Scunthorpe. Taking poetic license in his description of the railway entrance to the town, which is via a cutting that did not allow for a panoramic view of steelworks, Lewis uses other familiar Scunthorpe areas, pubs where strippers entertained and the following street scene: *"I handed in my ticket and walked through the barrier. I looked round for a taxi. Nothing. Beyond that was the road with its loveless lights and its council houses. The cab swung into the car park. It was a strange place. Too big for a town, too small for a city. As a kid, it had always struck me that it was like a western boom town. There was just the main street where there was everything you needed and everything else just dribbled off towards the ragged edges of the town ... Thirty years ago, it had been just another village hiding in the lee of the Wolds ... Then they had found sandstone."*

The plot was as follows. Jack Carter worked for gangster brothers Gerald and Les Fletcher as an enforcer and heavy. They had many criminal interests, including distributing rollers, protection and fruit-machine rackets. When Carter discovers that his elder brother Frank had died in a suspicious car accident, contrary to the wishes of the Fletchers, he sets out to discover the truth. A sub plot is that Jack despised Frank's cowardice and appears to have fathered Doreen, the only daughter of Frank's marriage because of his contempt for Frank's cowardice. Jack investigates the 'Doncaster' underworld, leading him to flush out two local criminals, Cyril Kinnear and Cliff Brumby. Enter Eric Paice, Kinnear's chauffeur, but a former London enforcer with whom Carter had 'history'. Unknown to Gerald Fletcher, his wife Audrey is also Jack Carter's mistress. The Fletchers have secret criminal interests in Doncaster, however, so 'heavies' (Con and Peter the Dutchman) are sent to 'encourage' Jack to return to The Smoke before he finds out too much and his vengeance interferes with profits. Jack discovers the fifteen-year-old Doreen was 'pulled' by Paice to appear in a pornographic film distributed by Brumby. He sets about exacting revenge. He brutally murders the actor who seduces under-age Doreen in the porno film as well as Frank's mistress, the procurer. He beats up Brumby (in the film, throws him off the multi-storey car park in one of the most classic and well-known death sequences in British movie history) and then sets about killing Paice. The final sequences are set on a bleak estuary area with ruined brick buildings and ancient abandoned kilns, identical to The Old Cements of Lewis's youth. Jack and Paice fight to the death in the book, though this was changed in the film, but not before Jack has contacted a press contact to make sure the local police are aware of Kinnear's goings on, especially as he has placed the dead porno actress to be found in Kinnear's grounds.

The main plot's weakness is Jack's early naivety, for he is at once portrayed as all-knowing and streetwise, whereas he fails to realise the connection between his bosses and the underworld in Doncaster. He would be expected to know this through having a special interest his home town as well as inside knowledge of the Fletchers operations. Ted Lewis provides Jack with narrative that is sharp, pithy, cynical and expletive-ridden, the language disguising any such weaknesses adroitly. He convincingly describes explicit scenes of filming sexual activity, savage violence, and death coming as an easy solution. *Get Carter* had its UK premier on 10th March 1971. The year was a momentous year for Ted Lewis, not only because of the book and film success but also because his second daughter, Sally, was born that year. From being flat dwellers, the family went to live in Essex between 1968 and 1971, and where Ted entertained friends, including Ron Burnett from his college days, who was still in the area and remembers staying in their thatched cottage. Ted and wife Jo later ventured into the purchase of a run-down Suffolk farmhouse, Hill Farm, Kettleburgh near in Framlingham in Suffolk. Not for Ted Lewis the traditional gangster territory of Epping. Ironically, Hill Farm was a short drive from where Suffolk-born Ian Hendry, who played Eric Paice in *Get Carter*, regularly visited his parents in Little Bealings. Ted Lewis was one of the few who could keep up with Hendry's prodigious drinking habits. Ted Lewis had arrived.

Chapter 17

Get Carter

Get Carter's excellent actors delivered quality, credible roles to a storyline that is both pithy and gripping. The casting was as inspired as the engagement of Caine. The previous successful star of *Zulu* and *Alfie* had become a seriously skilled and dedicated actor over may years of taking minor parts. He created a completely credible portrayal of killer who appeared to have no conscience, yet under the skin had his own vulnerabilities and fears. It is impossible to think of Jack Carter when reading the novel without a vision of Michael Caine. John Osborne played suave, cool, controlling gangster Kinnear with complete credibility and authority. Ian Hendry won an award for his portrayal of the weasel, Eric Paice. Bryan Mosley, also feted for his long run in ITV's soap *Coronation Street*, is lugubrious as bent businessman Cliff Brumby, who takes on the iconic description Ted Lewis gave in the book for Kinnear: *"the person fat men like to stand next to"*. Distinguished character actor Bernard Hepton plays the once-controlling but cowardly Thorpey. Alun Armstrong, with a future Royal Shakespeare Company, National Theatre and TV career, and huge respect in the profession, plays the naïve, beaten barman. Glynn Edwards is the cringing, dirty, old porno abuser. Geraldine Moffatt is Glenda, brother Frank's mistress. Casting the cash strapped Britt Ekland was a sop to the American market.

But for this quality, innovative film, Ted Lewis, as a novelist, could well be of much less account rather than being recognised as a revivalist of criminal noir in UK, which he undoubtedly is. Unfortunately, notwithstanding a well-documented artistic stature, even in his home town of Barton he is sparingly recognised unless you refer to *Get Carter* by name.

The film's budget was a measly £1M; a last throw of MGM's UK dice, it having announced that the film company was shortly pulling out of Borehamwood Studios. The first imperative was to establish a suitable location for the run-down backdrop that was essential to the story. Director Mike Hodges wished to film in an area with which he was familiar and in which he could have confidence. Speculation as to why

Newcastle upon Tyne was *Get Carter's* location of choice rather than Scunthorpe is easily resolved. Scunthorpe, Hull, Doncaster and other locations were becoming increasingly developed, whereas Newcastle, as director Hodges remembered it from a brief National Service visit, had not yet fully emerged from its industrial past. Its grime, industry and grit were ideal. In addition to selecting the location, Hodges also wrote the screenplay, which was later published in paperback form and it is also still available. Its pithy dialogue, though it did not quite match up to Lewis's sardonic, direct, earthy dialogue, runs it a close second and it retains many of the iconic quotations. Toby Eady is of the view that Lewis, in all his writing, *"didn't care a flying ..."*, whereas Hodges did have to pay some lip service to acceptability. Accordingly, there were virtually no cuts by the then censor.

In directing *Get Carter*, Hodges managed the kind of authenticity Ted Lewis had achieved in the novel by means of cameras picking out the rugged, enquiring, bored or raucous faces of the north. Extra, Tracey Star, engaged to attack the suggestive pub singer (Denea White) fondling one of her audience, was on the books of a local agent and was selected because she was said to have a 'history' with White, although in later interview White played this down. Hodges paid real boozers £5 a head, one of whom was a friend of Lewis's fellow student, Lance Waddell. Hodges later described the faces and figures as 'Hogarthian', for they certainly added authenticity. Viewers are indebted to Assheton Gorton, the forty-year-old production designer, for his atmospheric treatment of the Newcastle area and its sets, as well as Wolfgang Suschitzky, a determined, accurate and inspired photographer and cameraman. Suschitzky had already distinguished himself portraying the seedy underworld of London and was therefore a typical Klinger/Hodges choice. He used long lenses and hand-held cameras to recreate the narrative that Ted Lewis had envisaged in the original novel. Between those two and Hodges there emerged an inspired image of Carter travelling on the train reading a Raymond Chandler novel, in recognition of the author who had so inspired Ted. For example, gangster Kinnear's home, Dryerdale Hall, was the chosen location due to being a former, luxurious home of gangster Vincent Lander, *"the man who ran Newcastle"*. The Kray twins had once visited Lander after notoriously and rather foolishly having been driven ostentatiously north in twin Rolls Royces, intent on expanding their empire into profitable fruit machine or other rackets. Lander was later murdered at Dryerdale, another gangland score settled and another lowlife, Angus Sibbert, alleged to have been fitted up; even after his sentence, he was still protesting innocence.

Ted Lewis may have regretted that he was not engaged to write *Carter's* screenplay, but he was certainly realistic enough to know films do not often fully shadow their roots, and was reasonably content to appear on set without apparent complaint. He also had no experience in writing actual screenplays, although he felt it in his soul. On set he rubbed shoulders with the urbane, gentlemanly Michael Caine and accepted that the actor was masterfully playing the Jack Carter Ted had created. Reputedly, Caine had much time for Lewis and they were certainly pictured together on set. Later in life, Ted would proudly show the photograph of him and Caine boating together just for enjoyment. Many of the other *Get Carter* actors, such as Britt Ekland, had no need to be in Newcastle at all, as their scenes did not require location shots and money was tight.

Ian Hendry (Paice), had previously appeared in the TV series *The Avengers* as Dr David Keal, and whilst jealous at being overlooked for the part of Jack, he was superbly convincing as a doomed weasel ex-enforcer turned chauffeur. Hendry needed to be dragged from the pub onto the set where, reminiscent of Oliver Reed, his lines after drinking were unaccountably word perfect. Classic minor-part casting included smooth-talking John Binden as gangster Les Fletcher, portrayed in Jack's Return Home as *"immaculate, smoking a Sobranie, pale beige corduroy suit with a lavender shirt and a carefully knotted brown silk tie"*. Binden's acting ability was first discovered by director Ken Loach, although Binden also had another career as a minder; he was sometimes known as 'Biffo', for his fist accomplishments. Later he became a real but minor gangster (nicknamed 'The Guv'nor') as he later admitted. Allegedly, Binden was a repository for alleged compromising pictures of HRH Princess Margaret, which strangely were never found. Authenticity in overdrive!

Dialogue in *Jack's Return Home* is littered with earthy, obscene expletives, which, although less frequently in *Get Carter*, are spat out in conversation as often as cigarettes are lit and glasses of alcohol are refilled. Hodge also rubs the viewer's nose in roller performances of sleazy celluloid from the beginning. *Get Carter*, however, contains a unique cameo showing Caine, said not to have viewed such raw rollers before, expressing obvious shock, disgust and almost tearful grief as Jack Carter watches scenes that in reality amount to serious child abuse. This is entirely consistent with Caine's later actual real life campaigning against child suffering, but in real time it was superb acting. Sadly, Caine received no award for portraying Jack although he had received a BAFTA and Golden Globe for his earlier ground-breaking best actor performance of Alfie. Just as Caine has his own quotable quotes, *"She's in luvly condition"* and *"Not many people know that"*, so does Jack Carter in a sardonically witty script: *"You're a big man, but you're in bad shape; With me it's a full-time job. Now behave yourself"*, *"A pint of bitter ... in a thin glass!"* and *"You know, I'd almost forgotten what your eyes looked like. Still the same. Pissholes in the snow."* The last quote, turned into a graphic, adorned a public area in Hull College at its new premises on Wilberforce Drive for many months.

In *Get Carter,* Jack's angry self-doubt is limited, omitting that mirror of Lewis himself, whose dark moods, difficulty in writing without a glass in his hand and vivid recollections of youthful humiliations threw up those sensitivities and vulnerabilities. The use of Trinity Square, the multi-storey car park in Gateshead, was genius at work; it was used as the setting for the death plunge of Brumby to the bemusement of his two architects planning a top-storey night club. The Gateshead car park did have a planned night club, but it never operated. The final denouement in *Get Carter* is presented on a stark, shale beach redolent of Ness End in Barton, but instead shot on the chilly, bleak Durham beach at Blackhall (now a nature reserve). The scenes show Jack, having drowned Paice in whisky as Paice did to Jack's brother, Frank, then slaying the hapless chauffeur, whereas the book has Paice mortally wounding Carter with a knife before being the victim of Carter's dying discharge of the iconic shotgun. Unlike in the book, Hodges has Carter dying from a single shot from a contract hit man hired by Kinnear. This change arguably chimes more with reality than even Lewis's plot. In the novel, gangland boss Kinnear weakens to Jack Carter's threats, whereas in *Get Carter* Kinnear had a confident ruthlessness redolent of the real-life Richardson gang. James Moody was a hit man working at the time for both the Krays and Richardsons, although he favoured the latter, and was reputed as having driven Eddie Richardson from the notorious gun battle between the two gangs at Mr Smith's club in 1966. Moody's nickname was 'Big J'; the film pans to the gunman's finger ring with the initial 'J' on it. Despite firmly believing Moody to be responsible for several hit jobs, Scotland Yard could not pin anything on him. What did Ted Lewis know?

Although not receiving critical acclaim, *Get Carter* was a success with the public, but was only nominated for one British Academy Award; however, Ian Hendry won a BAFTA for best supporting actor. Britain had not, until then, been exposed to British writing describing so incisively a true-to-life, dirty, contemporary underworld with ruthless grit. Whilst Lewis's parents had enjoyed *All the Way Home and All the Night Through*, they understandably found it difficult to cope with the Jack's Return Home narrative, probably finding it difficult to appreciate its overt, foul-mouthed, salacious characters, as well as likely being concerned about their son's associates. Agent Toby Eady, whose judgment proved to be peerless, always made it clear that Return/Carter was a significant, ground-breaking novel of immense literary quality. The literary agent holds to this view today, re-enforced by his forty-five-year experience. *Get Carter* is feted as the best, or at least one of the best, crime thrillers of all time, depending upon which critic you prefer. The grey, wet Trinity Square car park has now been torn down, symbolic of a world, street scenes, social habits and attitudes that no longer exist. Even the car park in Scunthorpe that Ted Lewis used as a model for Brumby's demise has gone. Only an abiding concern about coerced sex and fear of organised crime remains.

The USA film industry clearly saw potential in *Get Carter*, for in 1972 *Hit Man* starring Pam Grier was released; a 'blackspoitation' version of the British film. Although the film was not a success, interest in the storyline was a significant accolade to Lewis. In 2000, after Ted's death, Toby Eady, on behalf of the estate, negotiated the film rights to *Jack's Return Home* again, now for the benefit of Ted's children. There was a remake of the film, this time starring Sylvester Stallone, who was unable to emulate Jack's character as convincingly as Caine. Much later, Stallone demonstrated a personal commitment by lending his support to a campaign to preserve that crumbling Trinity

Square car park in Gateshead. The original *Get Carter* DVD is still available and *Get Carter* has been republished. *Get Carter* has been a 2015 theatre production by Northern Stage, playing in Newcastle initially, followed by a tour that appropriately included Doncaster. The character of Jack Carter was also obliged to live on in Ted Lewis's two prequels. Sadly, whilst Ted Lewis did earn significantly from his early artistic endeavours, he squandered the money he received.

From this time on, hard boiled crime novels poured out aplenty with increasing freedom. Ted Lewis had released inhibitions and paved the way for wave of post nineteen-seventies crime novelists who follow and fete him.

Typical Ted Lewis sketches.

Ted Lewis on the set of *Get Carter*.

Ted Lewis's literary agent's offices.

Typical Soho watering hole.

Renamed *'Get Carter'*.

Spoof action with Ted Lewis as Jack Carter.

Iconic Trinity Square Car Park featured in *Get Carter*, at the demise of Cliff Brumby.

Ted Lewis publicity photograph for Michael Joseph novels.

Lila Harrison, friend and for thirty-five years a barmaid at The George and in Lila's Bar; a legend.

Bertha Lewis's house at 33 Ferriby Road, Barton, where Ted Lewis often stayed after 1974.

New Hall, Barton, home of Ted's friend Dr John Dickinson.

Ted Lewis's portrait of Nadine Dickinson, showing the River Humber and wide sky.

Ted Lewis wrote three *Z Cars* scripts.

Sketches of old Barton by Ted Lewis in 1979, commissioned by Dr John Ball, and donated by him to Barton Civic Society.©

Sketches of old Barton by Ted Lewis in 1979, commissioned by Dr John Ball, and donated by him to Barton Civic Society.©

Ted Lewis (second from right) as many will
remember him, – always a party goer.

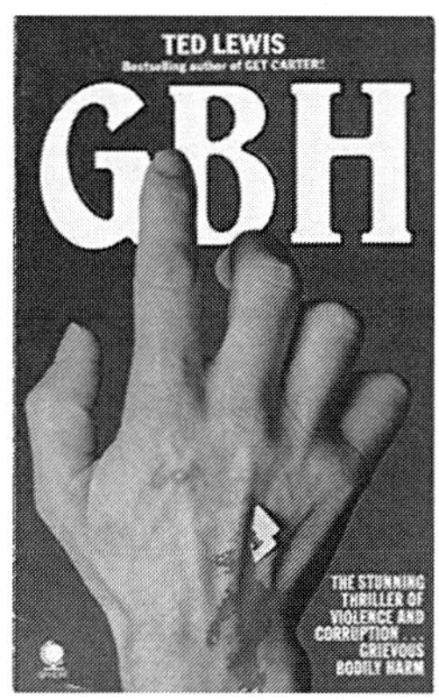

Ted Lewis's last two novels.

Ron Burnett, great friend
of Ted Lewis, still blowin'.

Chapter 18

Plender

1971

Elated by the acceptance and success of *Jack's Return Home*, and encouraged by Toby Eady, Ted Lewis embarked on series of novels that varied in subject and background, and which publisher Michael Joseph was only too pleased to publish. The first, *Plender*, £2.00 in hardback, was published in 1971, following *Get Carter* in quick time. The first chapter sets a scene familiar to Ted Lewis: *"A grey wet wind screamed up the Estuary and into the city centre, rocked trolley busses and swept old cabbage leaves along the grey cobbled streets Beyond the cranes I could see the broad river the colour of stone and across on the other, rural, bank ... three miles away, spare lights winked fitfully, delineating the flatness of the neighbouring county."*

Brian Plender was a seedy, criminally successful enquiry agent in Hull. He and Peter Knott, the other sleazy main character in the novel, had been neighbours in Barton, where both went to Barton Grammar School. Initially, it is not clear from the first chapters what plot is emerging, but, when it does, the story is nothing if not a little contrived. Brian Plender lived in an ordinary family home in Barton, much like West End Estate into which the Lewis family first moved. The Knott family become neighbours, but are a cut above the others (no-one confesses to being the model for this or points the finger). Brian Plender is stung by Knott's achievement and monopolisation of his friends, and is humiliated at school and at leisure. Later in life, against an undercurrent of blackmail and Hull's organised crime scene, Knott inadvertently causes the death of a girl during one of his habitual one-night sexual exploitations. Plender has followed Knott and steals the girl's body, then blackmails his former tormentor. Most of the action takes place in Hull and its surrounding area, just as *All the Way Home and All the Night Through*. Whereas Ted Lewis's first novel describes Victor meandering with his girlfriend along Hessle's lazy Humber Estuary foreshore, in *Plender* it is bleak Sammy's Point, where the River Hull conjoins with the Humber estuary, that is the setting for Brian brutalising a defaulting blackmail victim: *"Bells rang and the Ferry began to chug away. Lank grass fell over my face. The*

Ferry passed by … I wished I was on board and seventeen again … The other man hit the man in the raincoat … and he fell to the ground vomiting."

The novel is told from the alternating vantage points of both Plender and Knott in a similar sequential style to Lewis's storytelling in his last novel, *GBH*. *Plender* also contains graphic, self-obsessed flashbacks to schooldays in Barton. Brian Plender is gulled into a supposed tryst behind the school pavilion and the ritual introduction to mutual masturbation, which has echoes in the sexual gang violence inflicted on Jackson in *The Rabbit*. We may never know the root of these events, contrary to the record of Ted's humiliation at the hands of headmaster Norman Goddard when Lewis wet himself, which has provenance. Fascinating to those closest to Ted Lewis in his youth was the passage in *Plender* when Brian overhears Knott's mother say to her son Peter, *"you've got to better yourself … lads like Brian … I've nothing against him … but … that'll just hold you back. They're no good to you."* Brian hears this as he is in the bathroom above the living room, the home configuration identical to Ted's home at 46 Westfield Road.

Although *Plender* did not have the success of *Carter* in the UK, it was translated into French and published by Payot & Rivages in 1996. The basis of the novel captured the imagination of the French and Eric Barbier wrote and directed the film *Le Serpent*, released in 2006, which was based on *Plender*; Ted Lewis is shown on the credits as a writing source. Dying in 1982, Ted Lewis never saw the film and we will never know what he thought of it.

Chapter 19

Billy Rags

1973

Writing now in Suffolk, the novel *Billy Rags* (£2.00, also published by Michael Joseph) followed *Plender*, two years later in 1973. The plot is told in the person of reckless and psychopathic criminal Billy Cracken, or 'Billy Rags', although this was not a nickname you would dare to use given his explosive violence. It is instructive that, in his young days, Billy Cracken is portrayed as having been humiliated in a fight; Ted Lewis returning to a familiar theme of victimisation. We meet Billy 'inside' (portrayed as *"Burnham"* prison – again a name taken from the Barton area), which is described with uncanny accuracy before the 1974 British TV sitcom *Porridge* was screened, and which accurately drew its humorous exaggeration from true life inside. Whereas *Porridge* allows the viewer a glimpse of the underworld hierarchy that continues from gangland to prison, Ted Lewis clearly describes the grit and angst of prison society, including the raw and destructive feelings of prisoners. Billy plans and executes a dramatic breakout from prison just two months before his sentence was due to end. We are treated to the privations of life on the run and the fragile loyalty of Billy's wife, knowing of her husband's predilections and the suffering he causes her.

The plot seems to have been triggered largely from the experiences of a real-life underworld armed robber and reputed 'public enemy number one', John McVicar, who had escaped from prison several times and was recaptured by the Metropolitan Police in 1970. McVicar was paroled in 1978, five years after *Billy Rags* was first published, and has become an author and journalist. McVicar was, however, paid a consultation fee via his wife. However, Ted Lewis also knew Bartonian contractor and scaffolder Billy Dickinson, who had become a drinking partner. That man had the unmistakable personality of the main character in the book, as related by friends and Billy's former wife, who record similar brittle domestic relationships. Although Billy Dickinson was not a gangster or career criminal, he had been to prison and had scant respect for the law or anyone else who got in his way. He could be entertaining if he wished, but also dangerous when upset or, as often was the case, when alcohol had the better of him. Billy Dickinson ranks with several other 'Barton characters' in Ted Lewis novels, including Big Tess who you crossed at your peril, Clacker the sardonic quarryman Teddy Boy, The Star cinema's officious owner "strutting down the aisle" and many others. Ted wrote in 1968 that *"You have to be ruthless ... If it means exploiting people well – it has to be done."*

Chapter 20

Jack Carter's Law

1974

Neither *Plender* nor *Billy Rags* achieved the popularity of *Get Carter*, into which *Jack's Return Home* had completely morphed. A noir style of criminal action novels had been in Ted Lewis's blood from his youth and it had proved to be his major success, so Ted wrote *Jack Carter's Law*, which was a prequel to *Get Carter* and also published by Michael Joseph (this time selling for £3.00) in 1974. The tough, sometimes brutal, man-about-town enforcer, Jack Carter, already had his character well established. A trailed summary of the novel is succinctly set out in the flyleaf to its first edition and cannot, in faith, be improved upon: *"It's Christmas Eve in London and all's quiet save for the whispering of grass. Now there's one thing Jack Carter can't stand, it's a grass* [informer] – *especially as Jimmy Swan is about to put him and his mates down for a twenty year stretch. The answer's simple: shoot him before he shoots his mouth off ... the return of the long-awaited return of the smartest, sexiest villain in the business."*

Ted Lewis's harrowing description of the abuse of women is a consistently alarming but essential feature of his writing going forward. This time violent, casual yet expected; *"I down my drink and go over to her and give her one round the ear-hole that sends her glasses flying,"* says Carter. There was more extreme violence from the fists of gay thug Peter the Dutchman, who first appears in Get Carter, as does Con McCarty and the Fletcher Brothers. It is difficult to divorce the words from the graphic portrayal of this Peter the Dutchman by Peter Beckley, arrayed in his white mac and sunglasses, who also appeared in Get Carter. Carter finds the girl subdued by a casual beating as follows: *"A broken sound that is hardly loud enough to be a sob ... Lesley lying on the floor ... There are three or four bruises on her back. Her bottom lip is split completely and three of her top teeth are missing. One side of her face is the colour of charcoal ... Mallory pulls his hand back ... she screams again and wriggles like an eel."* The novel also introduces readers again to the blatant corruption of the Metropolitan Police, picking and choosing which villain to stitch up, and which to protect. Financial and sexual rewards were the currency, earning the contempt of Jack Carter who, we might cynically suspect, might have behaved in a similar fashion if his career had started in a blue serge uniform.

There is a sterile argument as to whether Ted Lewis intended to embark on a career solely as a crime writer following *Jack's Return Home*. The reasoning is that, initially, he had written *All the Way Home and All the Night Through* with an entirely different emphasis, so why should this not have been his initial path in literature? When asked by media or literary commentators and critics, his responses were characteristically ambivalent. Wife, Jo, thought he did not set out to be a crime writer, which is probably correct, but he did set out to write about what he knew, finding that his style and in-depth knowledge of thrillers suited the subjects with which he was fascinated. His characteristic Barton style of language flowed easily, which was a bonus to a notoriously ill-disciplined writer. Whenever he felt reality in fiction was necessary, he would have no hesitation in relying on those details of his earlier life or experiences.

Chapter 21

Return to Barton upon Humber

1974

By 1973/4 Ted Lewis's marriage to Jo was, sadly, in trouble. The family was still living in that old Suffolk farmhouse that Ted had purchased when financial as well as artistic success was his for the taking. Many commentators assert that Ted's marriage broke up with pint glass in his hand at home, but wife, Jo, later went public to qualify this. His singular ways as well as pressures from overstretched building operations to the farmhouse, which became a bottomless pit, contributed to domestic tensions. Whilst Ted would not exhibit a truly prodigious consumption of alcohol at home, he would sneak out to the pub and knock back an eye-watering amount, especially gin. He would build up bar bills of Oliver Reed's epic proportions and was unable to cope with any form of record keeping, eventually becoming too scared to visit his otherwise helpful bank manager. Jo suggested a separation for the protection of Nancy and Sally in the hopes that Ted would come to his senses, but this did not happen. Because of a need to sustain finances, just before his return to Barton in 1974, Lewis wrote a Jack-Carter-based, little-known short story, which was published in the Christmas edition of the UK 'gentleman's magazine' *Men Only*, entitled *Kings, Queens and Pawns*, adjacent to a photo of a bare-breasted model of ample proportions. He also wrote an also a somewhat far-fetched but compelling story for *American Club Magazine*, which showed the legend on its front page *'Not to be sold to persons under the age of eighteen'* as well as trails for *'Dial a Hooker'* and *'Pubic Hair Styling with Middle Parts'*. Lewis was creeping into and becoming, for the moment, part of the sleaze of which he wrote objectively in other works.

By the time Ted returned to Barton, the family had downsized to the terraced house at number 20 Westfield Road, less than 100 yards from the home at number 46 which he had lived. Father, Harry, had retired in 1971 and had died of lung cancer, with Bertha by his side, at home on 9th April 1975, shortly after Ted's return. The novelist had been trying to cope with contact in respect to Nancy and Sally, and there were some visits of the children to Barton and Ted to

Ipswich, where he had to stay in a hotel. However, as drink tended to play an inappropriate part in the proceedings, Jo put her foot down. She realised that Ted was not going to change and issued divorce proceedings, which were quickly finalised. She stayed at Hill Farm for another three years before finally leaving. Bertha sold 20 Westfield Road after Harry died and further downsized to 33 Ferriby Road, a terraced house some 400 yards away.

Barton was, naturally, quite different in 1974 from 1961. Although still playing lip service to its self-sufficient form, it was increasingly without means of industrial or craft support; where three supermarkets could unaccountably trade side by side with three High Street butchers; where no one had a good word for the town or its council; where youth roared round the roads more mindlessly; and where new-built houses said goodbye to their breadwinners in the morning only for them to return, complaining that there was nothing to do in the town at night. Even the Oxford cinema had become a bingo hall and the corner site of The Star was an embryo supermarket. Barton was no longer in Lincolnshire politically, but in newly created Humberside, which sat astride the Humber Estuary that Ted used to cross by ferry years before. A bridge, which many swore would never be built, started its inexorable construction the same year 'Ted Returned Home'. When completed, it was the longest single span bridge in the world and transformed north/south bank travel. The Humber Ferry was withdrawn on 25th June 1981, a part of Ted Lewis's life, which between 1956 and 1961 was an important focus. Offices on Hull's Victoria/Corporation Pier (the pier head), also graphically described in both of Ted's autobiographical books, became disused as later did the Humber Pilot Office in the same area. On 17th July 1981, Her Majesty Queen Elizabeth II officially opened the Humber Bridge.

The Hull fishing industry was in terminal decline causing James Johnson, the West Hull MP before John (now Lord) Prescott, to declare in Parliament *"I came to Hull about 20 years ago, and found well over 130 boats in the dock, with well over 600 bobbers or dockers to unload the fish. This was a place of cheerful noise and jolly activity, despite the low wages that the men received. The landings were well over 200,000 tons, mainly of cod and haddock. Today, there is one vessel landing in the dock in a fortnight."* Redbourne Mill on

Normanby Park, Scunthorpe sadly ceased production in 1977 when British Steel made over four thousand redundancies; the whole area falling silent to reclamation by the early 1980s. When *Get Carter* was made in 1970, a new, modern Anchor Steel Works site was being built in Scunthorpe as preparation for rationalisation. The construction work ironically provided its own seed bed for local corruption as later criminal trials testified.

Ted had many friends and drinking acquaintances in Barton, but none of whom treated him as famous or hardly ever alluded to his gifts as a musician or artist. He gave himself no airs and graces. He tinkled on the few pianos that remained in pubs. Apart from those who were close or received sketches from time to time, most had little grasp of who Ted really was. Before the final divorce his pretty, blonde wife, Jo, had generally been liked by those she met in Barton during earlier happier days, and Bertha had visited them in Suffolk. Although Ted plainly loved his young children, regretting his marriage's demise, they were not much of a part of his final life in Barton. Instead, the charmer, a magnet for the ladies, a womaniser to some with bedroom eyes that could make a lady feel the most special in the world engaged in a variety of live-in and extra relationships with several who are still living and whose privacy, as with divorced wife, Jo, it is proper to respect. Ted lived first on Holydyke in Barton, ironically asking Jo how she would feel if he lived with a woman and three children. He later moved on to other dalliances, to Glebe House on Whitecross Street, for a time in the nearby village of Theddlethorpe, Barton's Overton Court and Priestgate, finally and ironically feeling unreasonably rejected and dejected. In between dalliances he would live with his mother, Bertha, in the modest terraced house at 33 Ferriby Road, Barton, also borrowing money from her for drink. He was living partly there and partly at 13 Overton Court in his last days.

Ted's problem was that the testosterone gremlin sitting on his shoulder was more powerful than his self-control. He first described in *All the Way Home and All the Night Through* that inner compulsion to use charisma for sexual conquest just because he could. After finally accepting that his romance to Janet was over, Victor Graves returns to Barton and attends an annual bonfire event: *"I was standing next to the trestle table where some of the Cons girls were dishing up hot peas and cartons of peas … I was served by a girl called Monica. I'd been friendly with her at school, and after, but nothing more. 'Monica, how would you like to come for a drink with me?' … 'All right, all right, why not?' … We reached the car … It had all been said* [later in the pub] *to take my mind off Janet … She drove the car off the road …'Vic' she breathed, 'Vic, Vic'. I pushed my hand inside. 'Vic, because of what I said – don't think I'm easy.'*" For Victor, aka Ted Lewis, it was easy.

Chapter 22

The Rabbit

1975

In 1975, *The Rabbit* was published also by Michael Joseph, this time at a price of £3.75. Ted wrote lyrically again of his young life in Barton upon Humber, as personified by alter ego Victor Graves who featured in *All the Way Home and All the Night Through*. Ted Lewis made some mistakes in the street-scene events, which suggests that those parts were written before he returned to the town. The Victor Graves of *All the Way Home and All the Night Through* appears again, the same self-absorbed account of his romance with Janet at the college, but also being humiliated at his father's quarry during a holiday job. Their principal work was to chip flints out of the quarried chalk so it could be used effectively. Ted and his friend Nick Turner had, in their holidays, taken a holiday job at Elsham Quarry so had a shared experience, not only with each other but with Victor Graves, hero of *The Rabbit*. There he encountered hard-bitten, often taciturn workers whose copious drinking young Victor Graves tried to emulate. Victor found himself unable to match them pint for pint, fist for fist, just as he felt Jack Carter might have acted.

This is the novel in which the poignant account of Victor wetting himself in public at school appears. Early sexual experience is described graphically, and a male rape scene, observed awkwardly by Graves and which falls short only of penetration, is truly disturbing. The capacity of a Barton acquaintance in raw carnal desire at a wood yard shows Lewis wonder at an easy sexual conquest by a disrespected youth. This is a fascinating book for Bartonians, describing people and places many were familiar with. For that reason, Ted kept a stock of the hard-backed books, which he gave away selectively to a chosen number. After Ted's untimely death, Allison & Busby, which had republished Get Carter in 1992 and held the rights to do so until recently, published a reprint of the novel in 1998. In real time, Ted lapsed into becoming a prodigious and regular drinker in Barton pubs, some of which no longer exist. However, many of Ted's regular haunts remain, particularly The Wheatsheaf, Blue Bell, The George Hotel (now Inn), Red Lion, White Swan and Volunteer Arms. In the case of the White Lion, only a sign has existed for some time, and that has now disappeared although you can see where it hung.

Chapter 23

Boldt, Television and GBH

1976 to 1980

Ted Lewis continued to write after he had returned to Barton, as usual in a familiar, haphazard way. Much of his money had run out, but he still had a wife and two young children to support in Suffolk. His drinking and smoking soon developed into epidemic proportions and he was also from suffering from pulmonary debilitation, so doctors began to be concerned for his health. None of this made for a stable scenario for creativity. He was, however, a journeyman writer after all, so he buckled down and wrote *Boldt*. Agent Toby Eady had spent some time in the USA and this may have influenced Ted in creating a new character. US cop Roy Boldt, no stranger to 'the take' of corruption and cynically streetwise, together with his slightly less streetwise partner are engaged to ferret out any undercover plans in the criminal underworld to assassinate a visiting politician. The caricature for the hit man was a character called Albert Styles, the epitome of real-life British gunman for hire and model for Jack Carter's assassination, James Moody. Seemingly, all the characters in *Boldt* are either corrupt, double dealing or super sleazy. Roy Boldt is on the cusp of beating the system and escaping to anonymity when ... well, we won't spoil the story. Critics say *Boldt* competes with *Jack Carter and the Mafia Pigeon* for the title of weakest Ted Lewis novel, but both are stark noir accounts of the unacceptable, and so consistent with the Lewis style. Roy Boldt does not have the panache, skill, humour or appealing sexuality of Jack Carter – or is the image of Michael Caine subconsciously too strong? *Boldt* was published in 1976 again by Michael Joseph, £3.95.

What of Scunthorpe? Lewis had not been able to restrain himself from using allusions to the steel town, for example the names (Cliff) Brumby and Thorpey refer to two of five small villages; Brumby and Scunthorpe having merged together create Scunthorpe Borough in 1936. In a similar way, Arnold Bennett immortalised the un-named Stoke-on-Trent from other historic areas as in *Anna of the Five Towns* (in real life, six towns). On Ted's return, Scunthorpe still included a mile and a half of lurid, dirty, brooding-but-productive steelworks, clearly identified by description in *Jack's Return Home*. However, after 1977 Ted Lewis never again published a work with a background of Barton or Scunthorpe, although at his death he was writing *Other People's Houses*, a novel never competed or published, which was about life in industrial North Lincolnshire homes and not, as used to be suggested, another Carter romp.

Chapter 24

Final, Awkward Times in Barton

During the final eight years he spent in Barton, Ted still presented as the quiet, often-withdrawn person, although he could unsurprisingly be awkward as people frequently are when drink takes over. John Walters commented accurately upon the effects of drinking in his acerbic portraits, *Feckers*, which alludes to some of the drinking excesses of the Irish: *"Alcohol is a mind-altering drug. The whole point of downing a pint is to do something to your mind – to reduce anxiety, to increase self-esteem, to shake off inhibitions and, in extreme cases, to achieve a temporary annihilation of the consciousness."* Lewis emulated all that. Dr John Dickinson, a partner in the group practice at Barton's Central Surgery, a building not having even been in existence when Ted was a young man, became seriously concerned. At his home, New Hall in Newport in Barton, Ted delighted John and Nadine by playing the piano when the mood took him, sometimes also entertaining others, often with jazz and blues, when he played in local pubs. He retained his love of jazz, particularly Charlie Parker instrumentalists apart from his piano influences. To both friends, Ted's music had bitter-sweet overtones of a talent that was becoming neglected through drink. Ted was well known for that addiction and another to cigarettes – an excess that those who loved him were powerless to limit.

His 1976 novel, *Boldt*, set in the USA, showed him straying well out of his experience, which was not Ted and, in consequence, the novel was not a success either in terms of sales or literary interest, but now it is re-published views may be tempered with better acquaintance. However, now, Ted Lewis discovered another string to his bow. In 1975 he wrote *"Prisoners"*, his first episode of BBC TV's *Z Cars*, which was screened in January 1976. Maybe, if he could have succeeded in this genre of writing, Ted might have established a parallel career as a scriptwriter, providing another argument that he could have probably have successfully had written the screenplay of *Get Carter* instead of Hodges. Although, in 1962, *Z Cars* had been heralded as realistic and ground breaking, this Liverpool-based police series had developed a *Dixon of Dock Green* cosiness, in the banter of PC Jock

Weir and 'national treasure' Brian Blessed's lumbering portrayal of PC Fancy Smith. Later episodes of *Z Cars* had been given an injection of grit, which was more to Lewis's style. His episode of *"Prisoners"* in season eleven had been a useful introduction to script writing from Barton where, as a schoolboy, he had published in a school magazine that hoveringly dark school short story *Double Shuffle*, containing the lines, redolent of Jack Carter, *"impersonality struck him like a wall built of ice bricks. Aloneness surging round him from the neon lights, the arcades, he went into a bar the first night he arrived."* Lewis then went on to write two further *Z Cars* episodes, *"Juvenile"* in 1977 and *"Driver"* in 1978. This work might have continued, but the whole show ended in 1978 after eight hundred and three episodes.

Interspersed between writing episodes of *Z Cars*, Lewis wrote *Jack Carter and the Mafia Pigeon*, published in 1977 by Michael Joseph (with a price of £4.25). Its title and background, as in *Boldt*, appears also to have been influenced by Toby Eady's six-year residence in the USA. The plot is the unlikely account of a USA hoodlum, Joe D'Antoni, who, despite the Mafia omertà bond of silence, had given valuable information to enforcement agencies and was consequently dubbed a 'stool pigeon' ('grass' in English slang). Joe's only immediate future was assassination, hence the eponymous *Mafia Pigeon*. He is given unlikely sanctuary in Les and Gerald Fletcher's remote villa in Spain, and it is to this unlikely spot that, unwittingly, the otherwise all-knowing enforcer, Jack Carter, was sent, ostensibly to take a holiday. Despite this being a fanciful scenario and Jack's naïvety being a hugely more obvious flaw than in *Get Carter* days, the enforcer remains sardonic, socially critical, effective and sexually promiscuous. In this second and final prequel to *Get Carter*, Audrey, the wife of Jack's employer gangster, Gerald Fletcher, appears, and the plot seems to echo how obviously foolish such a catastrophic relationship must have appeared from the start. Lewis was minimally travelled, hence he gives Jack Carter a fear of flying and describes little of life abroad, especially neglecting graphic Spanish topography or the country's way of life. As in *Boldt*, Ted Lewis's inexperience of the USA made a cardboard cut-out of stool pigeon Joe, and for all those reasons the novel is not Lewis at his best, including the nadir of Lewis's work in its accounts of brutal, gratuitous, violent treatment of women.

In 1978, no doubt because of his promise demonstrated in *Z Cars'* scripts, Lewis was delighted to be commissioned to write four episodes of BBC TV's science fiction series *Doctor Who*, season sixteen, *"The Key to Time"*, with Tom Baker cast as The Doctor. Ted Lewis wrote these at a time when drink was becoming more of a problem to him and others. Friend and barmaid Lila Harrison recounted how she picked him up out of the alleyway that gave access from the rear of The George to the front of the hotel. She took him back to the family home in Priestgate where she and her husband lived, some 75 yards away, and there he slept around the clock, out of it through drink. Her son John also had to revive a collapsed Ted Lewis in Barton's Market Place the same year, just two examples of a drinking habit that was out of control. Added to that problem, science fiction was out of Lewis's life experience, so he wrote one of the main characters in Carter style, which was inappropriate for the traditional behaviour and ethos of The Doctor. Consequently, his scripts were rejected. Giant of sci-fi, Douglas Adams, wrote those episodes instead, but Lewis was crushed not only at having thrown away a golden opportunity but more so because his skills had not been appreciated.

Back to the typewriter, Lewis then wrote his last novel, *GBH*, which some critics consider Ted Lewis's best hard-boiled work. It has tension, suspense and dark fears in contrast to the trite environment of a desperately quiet, out-of-season Lincolnshire seaside town: *"In Mablethorpe they open at ten o'clock in the season or out of it ... The South Hotel is a hotel in name only ... in Mablethorpe there are boarding houses only ... The whole town is just the sum of parts of its buildings."* The novel is told in the first person by gangster George Fowler, who is hiding out in his Lincolnshire bungalow hideaway, evading enemies who are trying to take over his criminal empire. Only Ted Lewis could have featured the unlikely 'Kiss Me Quick' joke of a town as a location, but he does so with skill and conviction. George (Jack Carter in 1980s clothing) has prepared his hideaway bungalow with *All-Night-Long* style, including a split-level, 1960s-style living room complete with trendy gadgets. Nevertheless, it is the best hard-boiled noir novel since *Jack's Return Home/Get Carter*. Who is the mystery girl? Who is trying to take over the action in The Smoke? Who will get to Fowler before he gets them? Ted Lewis peppered the text with nice asides like *"another stupid thing was that he was a*

Millwall supporter." Lewis quirkily touches base with his previous writings such as *"'turn left at Plender Street', I said."*

There is no record of any Ted Lewis newly written published print after that time. Until 1982, Lewis continued his life drifting around pubs, playing on the piano in the Red Lion, sketching for fun, or for those he drank with or cared for. He enjoyed the company of musicians Nick and Diane Cardee, with whom he played, drank and turned his hand to composition. Anecdotes abound concerning escapades connected to good nights out; for example, when Barton Beck was flooded he determined to cross it on the way home, but halfway across realised he could not swim. He joined the Blue Bell darts team organised by Mally Speck, not to take part in matches as his playing was not renowned but because it would involve many visits to other pubs. These are all kindly reminiscences. Ted Lewis was still charming and courteous when this quality was not overtaken with excess. When depressed, though, he would take to the pub piano, and play dirges and marches; the customers urging him to brighten up the repertoire.

Ted's poor health was under regular medical supervision and Dr John Ball also befriended him. The doctor had come to Barton in 1961, the year Ted left, and was senior partner of Central Surgery's General Practitioners Group. Ball was known as a man of energy, particularly for amassing his huge pictorial record of old Barton upon Humber, on which he was a recognised authority. Out of kindness as well as interest, Dr Ball commissioned down-on-his-luck Ted Lewis to sketch eighteen old pictures and postcards of the town. Bertha recognised that it took Ted's mind off drink when concentrating on work in which he still had pride. Ball paid Ted £100, a sum worth vastly more than today, and then generously donated those drawings to Barton Civic Society. They were later recovered by Barton Arts, framed by The Ropewalk Arts Centre, and are available for display at Barton's Victorian heritage Wilderspin National School when not carefully stored. Atheist Ted Lewis was, by this time, seeking some spiritual help or belief, and spent some time helping a priest in his Scunthorpe church.

Ted never produced a piece of public art after 1980. At Scunthorpe General Hospital on 27th March 1982, aged forty-three years, Ted

Lewis died prematurely of alcohol related illness. The funeral was held in Barton on 5th April 1982 attended by Jo, Bertha, Drs Dickinson and Ball, and local friends, licensees, those with whom he had relationships, and musicians, but seemingly none of his London associates. His body was cremated; the authority for which was not from his mother who had been his rock in Barton, but by his then girlfriend, Jean Collingwood in Overton Court. He was survived by Bertha, Jo, Nancy and Sally, and, of course, his many ladies. His idol, Raymond Chandler, had also died of alcoholism the year before. Jo received her former husband's limited belongings, including chapters of his latest writings. Letters of administration of his estate were not taken out by his daughters until 1996, extracted by local Barton Solicitor, Keith Ready. In consequence, no literary executor was appointed so Toby Eady was engaged to negotiate contracts exploiting Ted's intellectual property. Bertha died on 13th February 1990 of a heart attack. Her final home was at 17 St Peters Court, a block of small flats converted by the Local Authority from the former town council offices. She outlived her husband by twenty-five years and her son by eighteen. She had been loved and respected by many, especially in her capacity as a school secretary at Barton's Bereton School and in her sweet shop. The Barton homes she lived in over forty-four years were within quarter of mile radius of each other and, after leaving her native Lancashire and her mother joining the family, became a real Bartonian. In later life, as her son had as a teenager at 46 Westfield Road, she had a hand in productions of fictitious drama, although they involved larger casts than her son had. She was as loved and well respected as was her son, but Ted had the wider and larger cast in the short run of his life, many of those members living immortally through entertaining novels.

Chapter 25

What Later

After 1982

Allison & Busby re-published several of Ted's novels after Michael Joseph. Peter Day, who was well respected in the literary world and who was instrumental in publishing Ted's first successful novel, moved to Random House of which Allison & Busby are a part, his death greatly mourned. Ted Lewis books then largely ceased to be popular and many went out of print. Ted Lewis's work inspired the 2000 Stallone film version of *Get Carter*, and, in 2006, *Plender's Le Serpent*. The men's magazine *Loaded* published a comic strip of Jack Carter and also an assessment of Ted Lewis novels in 2009, both of which served to interest more people in his work. Since then, there have been laudable efforts to encourage an understanding of Ted Lewis's major contribution to English literature. In 2009, Brian Greene from North Carolina, USA, literary administrator, writer and journalist, after alleging he had read all Lewis's novels at one sitting, penned several Internet articles in praise of the writer. He came to the UK, interviewed many people who had known Ted and received various artefacts after promising a self-styled 'official biography'. Meanwhile, journalist, writer, literary critic and lecturer from Barton, Nick Triplow, was researching and said to be rushing to first publication. Nothing happened, although at the time of writing we expect Nick's work is shortly to be published on eBooks but Brian Green decided he would not proceed with his. Nick Triplow cooperated in a short film *Ted's Return Home* (available on YouTube) for the Humber Mouth Festival, screened on 23rd July 2009, agrees that it is somewhat pedestrian. *Jack Carter's Law* was adapted for BBC Radio in 2010. Northern Stage produced *Get Carter* which toured theatres in 2016, adapted by Torben Betts.

Barton Civic Society has erected a plaque to identify 46 Westfield Road where Lewis lived his early life. The Ted Lewis Group has a programme to place other plaques on relevant premises connected to the author, and has published *Ted Lewis Trails*, which identify important places in Ted's life. In 2012, the BBC recognised the importance of Ted Lewis on the 30th anniversary of his death by recording *"Jack's Return Home"* co-presented by Newcastle-upon-Tyne University lecturer Sean O'Brien and Nick Triplow, but the podcast is no longer available. The Ted Lewis Group in Barton, revived from 2012, is determined to promote the writer's works and emphasise his importance. Friend of the Group, Alain Clément records that Ted Lewis novels have been translated into French: *Jack's Return Home* (as *Le Retour de Jack*) (1991); *Get Carter* (same title) (2001); *Plender* (same title) (1996); *Billy Rags* (same title) (2002); *Jack Carter's Law* (as *Jack Carter et la Loi*) (1996); *GBH* (as *Sévices*) (1993). US company, Syndicate/Soho Books has the rights to the republish the original texts on the initiative of enthusiast Paul Oliver, and has now published all the novels (for sale on Amazon as either paperback or eBooks); the reader of this biographical monograph is encouraged to read those works from which there have been short extracts in this book for understanding and study purposes. The object of this work is to further an understanding of Ted Lewis and the proliferation of his literature. Three exhibitions of the work, life and times of Ted Lewis have been mounted in Scunthorpe, Barton upon Humber and Hull (UK City of Culture). The Ted Lewis Group in Barton upon Humber, after promoting the artist for some years, has now been afforded facilities, in principle to create a monument and study area in Joseph Wright House in Barton to secure the memory of Ted Lewis.

Chapter 26

In Summary

The last defensive words were written by Jo, Ted Lewis's lovely wife, who still treasures the two chapters of the novel he was writing at the time of his death and that were delivered with his effects, saying, *"Ted had many qualities including immense personal charm. He was, however, tortured by self-doubt. His narrow-minded upbringing (being a writer was not a proper job), added to the guilt carried throughout his life, that eventually led him to chronic alcoholism … our daughters were born … we led a normal family life … those years were not spent in hard drinking."* There was nothing further, then, for her to add.

Ted Lewis was an innovative noir novelist, talented graphic and fine artist, entertaining pianist, and lovely man to so many people who treasure memories of him.

The Visit, No Return - What Might Have Been

The short story continued

I often wonder what would have happened if my hospital conversation with Ted had been more intuitive, informed or just plain more appealing. What if some of my words had lit up his milky gaze, which passed over me to the ward beyond, and had been animated, creative and stimulating? Perhaps we could have talked of a new barmaid at The Wheatsheaf; the price of beer in The George; of the coincidence that Jill, wife of Ted's pal Nick, was now working in my small Market Place restaurant; how Barton had changed; how Soho had changed; how Ronnie Scott's hadn't; and whether my hero Tubby Hayes was ever off drugs when he blew there. Then Ted might have told me anecdotes, times when he spoke to that enormously talented tenor player at Scott's. Oh yes, and we'd have talked of pretty girls, proposing also, but unconvincingly, that we might drink less. Ted would be dying for a smoke. We would agree to meet in the Red Lion when he hoped to be discharged the following week.

Ted's eyes might lazily begin to focus on a Maltese nurse whose enveloping sienna eyes I noticed had lit on him more than once. We would talk some more nonsense until I would detect, close by, a light perfume - Nina Ricci I think - realising quickly that it heralds a presence of the Maltese. She clearly does her own thing too. There comes an unmistakable look signalling that our visiting time at last is over. Glancing back, I would see the Maltese fuss round Ted's bed. Dr Ball is striding along, optimistically telling me how hopeful he is that Ted's treatment could succeed if followed carefully. The good doctor should have told his face as well.

After Ted died I slowly worked through regrets – what might have been. So, following Ted's example, I tried putting down on paper actual things that happened, the ones I believe were important; those that reflect, describe and commemorate the colour of his life as accurately as possible. Despite my scribblings, he still does live on more effectively in his novels and art.

Bibliography

Hodges M and Lewis T (2001). *Get Carter: Film Screenplay Classics (ScreenPress Classics)*

Davies S P (2014) *Get Carter and Beyond; The Cinema of Mike Hodges.*

Chisnall S (2003) *Get Carter.*

Triplow N (2014) *Tailpiece* to *Jack Carter and the Mafia Pigeon*

Collins M A (2014) *Preface* to *Jack Carter's Law.*

Walters J (2014) *Feckers: 50 People who Fecked up Ireland*

Greene B (2012) *Ted Lewis: No Maverick*

Greene B (2015) *The Grievous Life of Ted Lewis*

Greene B (2010) and (2014) *The Artistry of Ted Lewis*

Hodges M and Lewis T (1971) *Get Carter Film*

Spicer A and McKenna AT (2013) *The Man Who Got Carter: Michael Klinger Independent Producers with the British Film Industry1960 – 1980 (International Library of the Moving Image)*

Treece H (1953) *The Rebels*

Treece H (1949) *38 Poems*

Baggerley J A BA M.A. (Undated) *Henry Treece and the New Apocalypse: a Study of English Neo-romanticism*

Lavery B W (1915) The Headscarf Revolutionaries: Lillian Bilocca and the Hull Triple-Trawler Disaster

Philip Larkin and unknown contributor *Conquest Magazine by Brian W. Lavery (Author)*

Fisher M and Lines K (1969) *Three Bodley Head Monographs: Henry Treece*

Hall W (2006) *Sir Michael Caine: The Biography*

Bennett A (2006) *Untold Stories*

James H (1880) *The Madonna of the Future*

James Johnston MP *Hansard HC Deb 21 February 1979 vol. 963 cc585-94*

Josephine Lewis and unknown contributors *Arena Magazine*

Hearn MP (2012) Studio International Magazine *Celebrity Life at the Chelsea Hotel with Painter Michael Remfry*

Lincolnshire Life (various)

Education Act 1944

Various Authors (1954 (1955 (1956) The Bartonian

Dying for a Smoke (film) (1966-1968) http://www.screenonline.org.uk/film/id/1396616/index.html

Lone Ranger (film) (1967) http://www.bfi.org.uk/films-tv-people/50c307bad0d10

Wikipedia https://en.wikipedia.org *variously*, particularly wiki/Henry Treece; Ted Lewis; Jimmy Moody

Ted Lewis Novels – First Editions

All the Way Home and All the Night Through (1965)

Jack's Return Home (1970) (paperback published in 1971 as *Carter*. Later re-published as *Get Carter*)

Plender (1971)

Billy Rags (1973)

Jack Carter's Law (1974)

The Rabbit (1975)

Boldt (1976)

Jack Carter and the Mafia Pigeon (1977)

GBH (1980)

The quotations in the text of this biography which illustrate the life and times of Ted Lewis, often compared to the life of fictitious Victor Graves, have been taken from *All the Way Home and All the Night Through* and *The Rabbit*. Otherwise the novels are attributed in the text.

Ted Lewis – Magazine Articles

Men Only (Undated) *Kings, Queens and Pawns*

Club (Undated) *With This Song, Baby, It Don't Matter*

Posthumous portrait of Ted Lewis
by Barton artist James Usher

Ted Lewis Group, 1, Soutergate,
Barton upon Humber, DN18 5HG

frankiesatthirtyfive@gmail.com